chic metal

chic metal

modern metal jewelry to make at home

victoria tillotson

POTTER
CRAFT

NEW YORK

Published in the United States by Potter Craft, an imprint of the Crown Publishing Group,
a division of Random House, Inc., New York.
www.crownpublishing.com
www.pottercraft.com

POTTER CRAFT and colophon is a registered trademark of Random House, Inc.

Library of Congress Cataloging-in-Publication Data

Tillotson, Victoria.
    Chic metal : modern metal jewelry to make at home / Victoria Tillotson.
        p. cm.
    ISBN 978-0-307-40919-5
    1. Jewelry making—Amateurs' manuals.   I. Title.
    TT212.T57 2009
    739.27'2—dc22   2008019457

Printed in China

Design by Amy Sly
Photography by Marcus Tullis
Illustrations by Frances Soohoo

10 9 8 7 6 5 4 3 2 1

First Edition

For Lori Hollander,
my mentor and dear friend

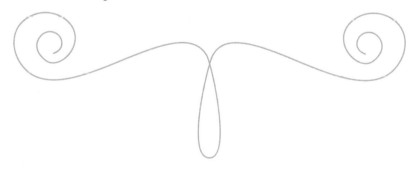

contents

introduction

It's happened to all of us. It's tragic, difficult, and frustrating: You search and search, and then you think you've found it—only to have the honeymoon end. It's burdensome, it's loud in public, it has no style, or it's simply unavailable. Or its personality is all wrong: It's shy when you're outgoing; it's boisterous when you want subtlety. In other words, it's just not quite right.

No, I'm not talking about the vicissitudes of dating. I'm talking about jewelry. See, finding the right person is pretty similar to finding the right jewelry. Here it is in a nutshell: You find the perfect outfit for an event. The dress, the shoes, the purse, the necklace and earrings—everything is working. You're in love and it feels great. Then, slowly but surely, you realize something is missing: Your jewelry, the link that should bring your outfit together and make you the star of the show, is all wrong. Admit it: No matter how adept you are at sniffing out that hidden treasure at the Barneys warehouse sale, landing that great pair of Manolos, or being first in line for the latest creation from Dior—or Abercrombie, for that matter—finding the right jewelry is the hardest and most heartbreaking aspect of any outfit.

This is where making your own jewelry comes in. The right piece of jewelry "makes" an outfit. In other words, it "makes" you—it defines your spirit, your personality, and your outlook on the world. The uptown girl dripping in diamonds makes a very different statement from the downtown chick rocking spiked earrings and a bracelet. Jewels are your signature pieces—so why not make one that really has *your* signature on it? Once you start making your own jewelry, you'll never look at jewelry shopping the same way again. Instead of buying it, you'll make it. And it will be uniquely *you.*

With *Chic Metal,* you can design and make your own beautiful metal jewelry simply and easily from your home, using basic tools and techniques. There's no fancy equipment to buy, and no complicated, boring directions. I show you different techniques, starting from basic to more challenging, that will enable you to create a whole jewelry wardrobe yourself. I also introduce you to tools you've never heard of and teach you to use some common tools in unusual ways. You'll never look at that chopstick, nail polish remover bottle, or frozen juice can in the same way again.

Some of the techniques you will learn are how to bend and manipulate wire with pliers, how to form and texture metal with a hammer, how to use a jewelers' saw, how to connect metal elements, how to add beads, and even how to "cook" your metal by soldering it with a mini torch, also known as a crème brulée torch. Finally, I'll introduce you to jewelry-specific tools like a ring mandrel, which allows you to make (you got it) rings and jump rings for chain mail and earrings, and a burnisher, with which you can set stones. Along the way, I'll teach you the wonders of the Dremel, a handheld rotary tool that does just about anything, from grinding to polishing to cleaning the grout in your shower when you need to take a break from jewelry making. But first, I will show you how to set up a simple, professional workspace in your home, so you'll always be ready to work when the jewelry mood strikes, without creating a mess or consigning your TV or computer to a lonely corner of your home.

I've structured *Chic Metal* just as I structure my courses. Banish any ideas of lectures here— this is strictly hands-on learning. Each chapter begins with a simple project that introduces you to a new jewelry-making tool and skill, and adds in more tools as you go along. Subsequent chapters encompass more complicated projects and cool tools. I recommend starting your jewelry journey at the beginning of *Chic Metal* and working your way systematically through the projects, rather than jumping in the middle of a chapter. At the very least, begin each chapter with the first project so that you don't have to backtrack to a prior project to figure out what's going on. My goal is success in jewelry making, not frustration or—sigh—failure.

Now, you may also notice that I've included a lot of earring projects in *Chic Metal*. Why? Well, for one thing I think of earrings as the most "universal" of jewelry styles. Who doesn't love a great pair of earrings? But for the nascent jeweler, earrings provide an excellent way to hone skills, as you *need to do everything in the project twice.* Going back to the success versus failure comparison, the more you practice a skill, the less likely you will be to fail. It's that simple. If you follow along with me, by the end of *Chic Metal*, you'll be able to successfully make and proudly wear your own designs, no matter what form they may take.

Yes, that's right. You can make cool, modern metal jewelry in your bedroom, your kitchen, your living room, your patio, or your backyard. *Chic Metal* will teach you how to embrace your inner do-it-yourself spirit, empowering you to create beautiful, wearable jewelry with simple techniques that can be adapted to your personal style. You'll learn how to create contemporary earrings, pendants, and rings that look professional and modern.

So break away from the "not quite right," the too-flashy, the too-tame, the shy, the loud, and the burdensome, and start creating your own perfect, chic metal jewelry.

bench basics

If there is one message I hope to convey, it's this: You don't need to have a studio or a workshop to make beautiful, professional-looking metal jewelry. I despise the common misconception that a jeweler's workspace is a haven of heavy machinery, whirring wheels, screeching saws, and pounding hammers. While many jewelry studios resemble hardcore workshops and have that type of equipment, just as many do not. People have been making jewelry for thousands of years in the tiniest of spaces without the benefit of hydraulic tools, or even electricity, so you can, too.

While my "professional" studio space is replete with drill press, polishing machines, grinders, mills, and cutters, my workspace at home is a 27" x 19" (68.5cm x 48.5cm) jewelers' bench. That's about the size of a large cutting board, a TV tray, or a small coffee table. On it is everything I need for most pieces I make—and definitely for all the projects in this book.

Since I have done this for so long in tiny New York City apartments—the corner of the crowded living room in one apartment, the foyer (literally) in another one—I have a few suggestions about how to create and structure a workspace that is compact, organized, and most of all, always ready for when the mood strikes.

1 Find an area in your home in which you can set up a small table or bench. The main thing is to create a space that is permanent and has one use—jewelry making. You should be able to leave your bench in whatever state it happens to be in at the end of the day. What type or size table isn't important; what matters is that it's sturdy and rugged. It will be beaten up. It will receive saw marks; its edges may be filed; it may become pitted with drill holes; and, if you're not careful, it may even end up with tiny burn marks when you solder. Choose something that can withstand this and, moreover, that you won't mind being a little worse for wear. Or think of jewelry making as a fun way to achieve that weathered, distressed look everyone likes. But be prepared: Your bench will get wrecked, so you have to be okay with this. (If you truly can't stomach this idea, a hardwood cutting board makes an excellent work surface and will protect your bench from much of the wear involved with jewelry making.)

An old-fashioned child's school desk works well for jewelry making, as does a used butcher-block table. A small jewelers' bench can be found from one of the sources in the back of the book. You can also check eBay.com or craigslist.org for a used one. A jewelers' bench can be expensive, so why not let someone else break it in for you?

2 You may find an ancillary surface next to your bench to be helpful. At home, I use a short file cabinet that I garbage-picked. On top, I keep my pickle pot (see Tools &

Supplies on page 12) and some tools, and I use the drawers for whatever I don't want to see at the moment.

You'll also need a chair. I use an adjustable office chair, but really, any one that fits comfortably with your bench will do. Many people also use a screw-type piano stool.

3 Start making coffee—no, not just to stay awake, but to empty some coffee cans. They are the perfect height and heft to hold many tools, such as files, pliers, or scissors. Put a couple of cans at the back of your table. If you set up your bench against a wall, you can mount a magnetic strip there to hold your tools, too. These can be found at cooking supply stores. Plastic stacking jars make good keepers for small parts. Flat Tupperware® storage bins are great for larger items and can stack neatly next to your bench or in a closet.

The tool glossary spells out the tools you'll need to make the projects in *Chic Metal*. Now you are ready to gather the bench basics, all of which you probably have around the house:

- Ammonia: Use in tiny quantities to remove any grease left over from polishing.
- Brad or other thin nail: For making holes.
- Chopsticks, pens, and/or wooden dowels: For making jump rings.
- Coat hangers: Great for inexpensive scribes. Cut them into 8" (20.5cm) lengths with wire cutters, and use a hand file to make points at the ends. Use when soldering or for scratching designs in metal.
- Frozen juice concentrate in a can.
- Glue stick and/or rubber cement: To glue paper models onto metal.

- Heat-resistant surface: To put a charcoal block on when soldering. Try a large ceramic dinner plate or metal cookie sheet.
- Nail polish remover: To remove permanent marker from metal. Plus the cap has a secret use . . . .
- Office supplies: Graph paper, tracing paper, round templates, permanent markers, scissors, pens and pencils, masking tape.
- Old ceramic or metal bowl: Use to hold water on your bench.
- Old tiny paintbrushes: For flux (see more in Chapter 3, page 84).
- Old toothbrushes: Use for cleaning.
- Pins: Yes, the ones used for sewing. Used in certain soldering techniques.
- Rags: I like to use old dishrags or terry-cloth bartender towels.
- Ruler: One that has measures in both inches and centimeters.
- Scotch-Brite® pads: Use to clean metal before soldering and to give a matte finish.
- Silver polishing cloth.
- Small Crock-Pot®: The little Crock-Pot used for dips will work perfectly. Use to warm the pickle solution for cleaning metal after soldering. Note: Once used for pickling, this Crock-Pot cannot be used for cooking.
- Tea ball: Preferably one that opens and closes by pinching the handles. For corralling small pieces when pickling.
- Your imagination: The most important tool of all.

tools & supplies

jewelry-making tools: what to buy and why

As soon as you become a convert to jewelry making and want to take your ideas far beyond the projects in *Chic Metal*, you will become an inveterate collector of tools. Many tools that advanced jewelers think of as routine and necessary are not so for the beginner. So, rather than overwhelm you with a comprehensive list of all jewelry-making tools, I've organized our tools into two lists—basic Needs and Wants.

Necessities come first, of course, then desires. The basics will enable you to make every project in this book (of course, the beginner projects require far fewer tools). Wherever possible, I have indicated alternatives to jewelry industry–specific tools you can use with similar results.

Needs

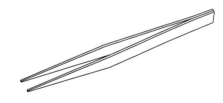

AA tweezers Long handles and sharp tips used to pick up small bits of metal and to place solder. You can get away with a good pair of personal grooming tweezers with a pointy tip, like those made by Tweezerman. But jewelers' AA tweezers are not only much less expensive but better.

Ball-peen hammer A simple metal hammer with a flat end and a round (or ball) end.

Beeswax A small bar of natural or synthetic beeswax used for lubricating a saw blade when sawing. A bar of soft soap, dishwashing soap, or a candle will work as well.

Brad nail Used with the ball-peen hammer to punch holes for ear wires.

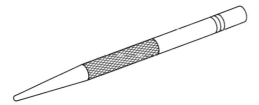

Burnisher A small, polished curved blade with a wooden handle, used for stone setting and smoothing metal.

Center punch A small pointed rod used to make a divot that acts as an initial anchor for a drill bit so it doesn't skitter around when you start drilling.

Charcoal block Please do not get a briquette from your grill! Jewelers need a small block of compressed charcoal on which to solder.

It reflects heat and concentrates heat, as well as protecting surfaces from flame—always a good thing.

Copper tongs Used for pulling pieces from the pickle.

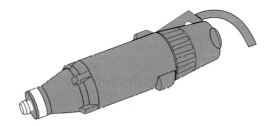

Dremel or flex-shaft High-speed rotary tool. A Dremel with a chuck accommodates grinding, drilling, and polishing bits. So useful you will wonder how you ever lived without one! A flex-shaft is a bigger and more comprehensive rotary tool. Resembling the drill used by your dentist (and maybe an instant turn-off because of this), a flex-shaft costs about four times as much as a basic Dremel. When you get serious about making jewelry, buy one.

Drill bits Used in the Dremel to drill holes in metal. While you can use drill bits made for wood, you will be better served by getting ones for metal. Make sure whatever you

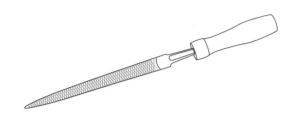

get is small—very small. Without going into too much technical detail or asking you to buy more equipment, unless your Dremel has a Jacobs chuck, you will need drill bits with a $\frac{3}{32}$" (2.4mm) shaft for use with a Dremel. This is a commonly found size and can be bought at jewelry supply or hardware stores.

Half-round hand file A hand file to be used on metal wire and sheet with a cutting surface of between 5" and 8" (12.5cm–20.5cm) long, with one flat side and one rounded side. Jewelers' files are sold without a grip, but you will want to get one to avoid fatigue and, over time, carpal tunnel syndrome. There are lots of variations, but get a simple and inexpensive wooden grip. Screw the file handle tightly into the grip.

Flux A chemical substance used to facilitate soldering by keeping the metal clean and preventing oxidation at the points at which it is to be joined. You can't solder without flux. It comes in different forms (like paste and liquid), but for now stick with the liquid form, such as Batterns®.

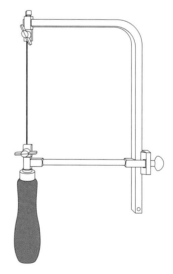

Jewelers' saw and saw blades A small hacksaw with adjustable frame, used with tiny saw blades (size 3/0 is the most universal).

Locking tweezers Cross-locking tweezers that have a spring in the center to hold a piece firmly. They come in all stainless steel or stainless steel with a wooden handle, which

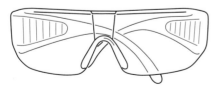

Goggles The safety glasses you wore in shop class. Goggles should *always* be worn when using a Dremel or other rotary tool.

aids in keeping the tweezers cool when you're soldering. Buy a couple of pairs—they are inexpensive and sometimes you need to use more than one in a project.

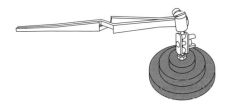

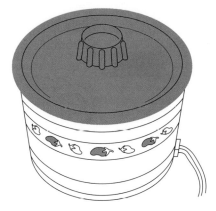

Locking tweezers with weighted base

Also known as a *third hand*. A metal weighted base that holds a pair of cross-locking tweezers. Used during soldering when you need to anchor a piece. A little obscure, but you will be infinitely glad you got one when I show you how to solder a ring.

Pickle An acidic solution used to clean oxidation and impurities from metal after it's been soldered. It is warmed up in a Crock-Pot before using. The most common brand is Sparex #2 (for non-ferrous metals like silver, gold, and copper).

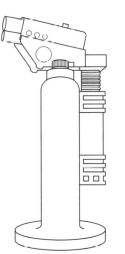

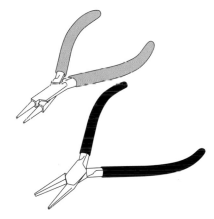

Mini torch A small butane torch with a fine, pointed flame used to heat up and solder metal. It is the same tool used in a kitchen to caramelize crème brulée. Believe it or not, this will work! But it's *much* better to get a jewelers' version, typically one made by Blazer. The quality is higher, and thus, it's safer.

Pliers Chain nose *and* round nose. Jewelers need two types of pliers, and it's worth it to seek out jewelry-making styles, which are machined and precise. Chain nose pliers are small metal pliers that are flat within the jaws with a rounded body that tapers to a point. Round nose pliers are small metal pliers with two fully round jaws that taper to a point. Pliers are available at a spectrum of price points, but there is no reason to spend more than $5–10 each at this point.

Polishing cloth Used as a final buff to remove any fingerprints or smudges from the piece.

Polishing wheels Made of coarse stone, rubber, or muslin/felt, these wheels are mounted to steel sticks (mandrels) and are used with the Dremel to polish your metal. For now buy a few blue silicone carbide rubber wheels that will be used as a first polishing step to remove marks from the metal, and a few felt and/or muslin wheels to use with tripoli and rouge to shine the metal.

Ring mandrel A tapered, round steel rod used to create rings by bending metal around it. Yes, it's industry-specific. No, you can't really live without it.

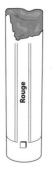

Rouge A greasy polishing compound that comes in bar form, used to give metal a

final, shiny finish. Used as the final step in a project.

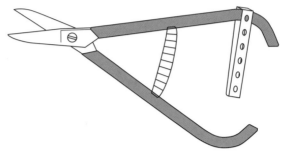

Shears Heavy-duty scissors to cut metal. There are industry-specific ones, but a pair of tin snips from a hardware store will do the work. I also have students who swear by Joyce Chen kitchen shears.

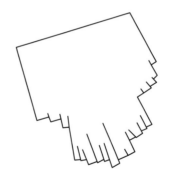

Solder A metal alloy used to fuse metal when heated. Typically (and confusingly) called hard, medium, and easy (or soft), names that refer to the melting temperatures of the solder, not to how strong they are. Hard has the highest melting temperature and is used for the first soldering step in a project. Easy has the lowest and is typically reserved for the final soldering step. I prefer sheet solder to wire solder. Sheet solder is labeled at the top as H, M, or S. It comes in small pieces about 1½" x 3" (3.8cm x 7.5cm) that you will then cut into tiny snippets of about ⅟₃₂"–⅛" (.75mm–3mm).

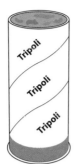

Tripoli A greasy, mildly abrasive polishing compound that comes in a bar or tube form. Used to shine and take light scratches from metal, and usually used after filing and sanding steps are complete before using rouge.

Wet/dry sandpaper Used for smoothing and finishing metal. Buy a couple of sheets each of 150, 220, 320, 400, 500, and 600 grit. Readily available at a hardware store.

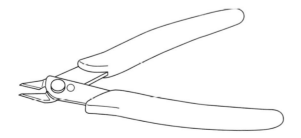

Wire cutters Sharp nippers with a small point used to accurately trim wire.

Wants

There are tons of tools out there, and at some point you will find yourself wanting *all* of them. I've stuck with some basics for now. Although this list is far from comprehensive, it's a good place to start.

Acetylene torch It's appropriate that an acetylene torch is the first tool on our list of desires. Your mini torch is wonderful and will serve you faithfully and beautifully for many, many soldering projects, but at some point, you will want a more efficient heat for creating larger pieces. Acetylene is a gas that produces a 2,400–4,500 degree Fahrenheit (1,482°C) flame temperature when combined with air. It is contained in a metal tank. Connected to it is a regulator that shows the amount of gas in the tank, a hose, and a handpiece that holds various size tips through which the gas flows and is controlled. Tiny tips yield a tiny flame and are perfect for small projects, while a large tip will allow you to work on that huge tribal neckpiece you've been hankering to make. Ask your local jewelry supply store for more information about the torch's use and precautions, and *be sure to learn from a pro* the proper way to set up, handle, and maintain the torch.

Bench block A heavy square of steel on which you can flatten and form metal. Also used when working with decorative stamps, to shape corners in metal, and as a coaster for a drink when your bench is too crowded. (OK, scratch the last use: It can rust).

Bench vise A small vise that screws into or clamps on to the end of your bench. Use to securely anchor projects. If you get one, buy a piece of rubber or vise pads like Soff Jaws to cushion the jaws so they don't mar your metal.

Bezel shears Tiny, precise shears that resemble children's safety scissors. Easier to use than large shears when cutting solder and very thin sheet metal like bezel wire.

Bracelet mandrel A large round or tapered stainless steel cone used to shape bangles and cuff bracelets. Big and heavy, it can serve as a doorstop when not being used for jewelry!

Dapping punches and block Sounds like a comedy team, but there's nothing funny about this amazing set of tools that is used to form and dome small sheet metal shapes by hammering the round end of a dap into a half-sphere cavity in the block.

Dividers Honestly, I wonder if I should not have just made these a "must." Dividers look sort of like calipers, and have two pointed steel "legs" with a fulcrum at the top and an adjustment screw to open and close the "legs." They are used to accurately measure, transfer distances when laying out work, and mark precise parallel lines in metal.

Magnifying visors Just as they sound. Most jewelers like OptiVISOR® binocular visors. If possible, try out a bunch in a jewelry supply or craft store to see which are best for you.

Needle file set Tiny, precise files that come in a variety of shapes. Indispensable when working with very small pieces or in tight spots.

Nylon jaw pliers For forming metal without leaving marks. A good alternative to wrapping chain nose or round nose pliers in tape.

Planishing hammer A jewelers' hammer used to stretch and form metal. Often has one rounded head and one flat head.

Rawhide hammer A hammer made of compressed leather. Used to shape metal because it won't leave marks as a metal hammer will, so polishing happens more quickly and easily.

Ring clamp A clamp that holds rings (and other small items) firmly in leather-lined, flat jaws. Typically double-ended and made of wood, it looks like a thick sausage with a V cut into it. Because a ring clamp provides a stable "handle" by which to hold your piece, it is excellent not only for holding a ring while setting a stone, but for gripping small pieces of metal while filing or polishing, eliminating finger fatigue and frustration.

Tripod and mesh A metal tripod with a piece of mesh that rests on it. Used when soldering pieces from underneath, and a nice alternative to locking tweezers with a weighted base when working on a larger piece.

jewelry-making supplies

This section is easy and short. You'll need some metal (and beads, if you like) to make the projects in *Chic Metal*.

Beads Gemstone, glass, plastic, or natural materials—the choice is yours.

Bezel wire Used to create the settings for stones in Chapter 4. Buy a couple of feet (60cm–75cm) of fine silver bezel wire that is ⅛" (3mm) wide.

Metal sheet The choice is yours. Metal typically comes in sheets of varying thicknesses. Copper and brass sheets are usually found in standard sizes, such as, 6" x 6" (15cm x 15cm), 6" x 12" (15cm x 30.5cm), 12" x 12" (30.5cm x 30.5cm), and larger. Sterling silver, though more expensive, can be bought in custom sheet sizes. Whatever you get, buy some in the following gauges: 28g, 24g, and 20g.

Metal wire Wire for jewelry is usually measured by "gauge," a measure of thickness. Whether it's copper, sterling silver, or brass,

buy wire in the different gauges: 28g, 24g, 22g, 20g, 18g, 12g. I will always use gauge to indicate thickness in this book for both sheet and wire, even though thickness typically is indicated in thousands of an inch or in millimeters. Ask the jewelry supply company from which you order to convert the measurement to gauge for you.

Premade elements Sterling silver ear wires, jump rings in various sizes, chain, and clasps are all examples of premade elements used in the projects in this book. If using copper or brass, buy jump rings and clasps in the appropriate metal. Ear wires should always be sterling, stainless steel, or, if you are using brass, gold or gold-filled because these metals are hypoallergenic.

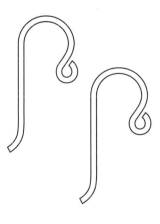

one

wire cutters, pliers, hammer, and file

Our first foray into silver jewelry making begins with four commonly known, commonly found, and decidedly non-threatening tools. Although humble, they are indispensable necessities in making any piece of jewelry, from the simple earrings in this chapter to a setting for a huge, sparkling diamond. Think of these tools as the workhorses of jewelry making.

Wire Cutters, Snips, Little Nippers

Whatever you call them, the name says it all. Hold and use wire cutters as you would pliers. It's as simple as that. Avoid using wire cutters on sheets of metal, as this will dull them and wreak havoc on the metal by compressing and distorting it. And it will take you a maddeningly long time to cut.

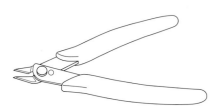

Pliers

These are not the pipe wrenches sitting in your garage. Pliers for jewelry are delicate, precise, and smooth where the blades touch. Hold them comfortably in the palm of your hand. When you pinch a piece of wire, use the pliers to anchor it while manipulating it with your other hand, rather than wrenching the piece around with the pliers themselves. You will make fewer marks in your metal this way, eliminating precious time spent polishing that could be better used on your next project.

For our projects, you will use two types of pliers—round nose and chain nose. Both are used for forming metal, and I will specify the use of each as we move along.

Hammer

We have all performed a task at some point using a ball-peen hammer (one side flat, the other, well, a ball). The hammering method for jewelry making is similar to that for hanging a frame: Always hold the hammer in your dominant hand. When forming or shaping (rather than texturing) metal, hold the hammer toward the end of handle. This way you generate more force. Train yourself to use methodical, even strokes. I recommend you practice hammering on a sheet of scrap metal, or go outdoors and hammer away on some wood. The trick to hammering is using even force and rhythm. Use the flat side of the hammer for molding and smoothing metal. The ball side makes a nice texture.

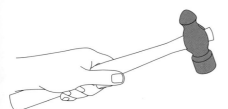

File

This is definitely not a good time for a manicure! Save that for later. But filing metal is pretty much the same as filing your nails in one direction. Hold the file as you would a knife by gripping the handle and placing your index finger along the top for control. You want to file in an even, forward motion. No sawing back and forth, if you can help it—this dulls the file. Think of the filing motion as touching the metal and gently moving the file along it by swooping your hand forward and then up and away from the piece. Methodical rhythm and patience are key here.

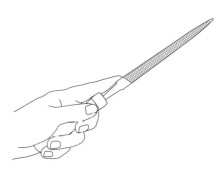

Another very important aspect of filing is to anchor the metal against a solid surface. Do not file with both hands up in the air! You will have no control this way. By holding your piece steady, you can concentrate all your effort on making good strokes.

Finally, a note about another important tool—patience. Call it Zen thinking, inner focus, whatever—the biggest mistake any jeweler can make is to rush through a project. At first, the desire for completion is so strong that you will want to cruise along at eighty miles per hour to the finish line. Slow down and go thirty miles per hour. Boring, yes, but entirely necessary. Patience is the hardest skill to acquire in jewelry making—really! I struggled with this at first, and every one of my students struggles with it. Those who become good jewelers fight the beast of impatience—and win. So whether you are making your first piece or completing a wildly complicated project, take your time.

long twig earrings

These earrings are a great way to learn how to hammer and shape metal. I love the long and lean look, inspired by . . . well, take a guess! The line of the earring is simple and timeless, but the hammering gives it a modern edge. Twiggies are perfect with jeans on the weekend but can also dress up an evening outfit with their sparkly faceted finish. Made with sterling, copper, or brass wire, they are easy and satisfying to make in any metal. The length and look of the earring depends on you, but I like ones that are about 2½" (6.5cm) long.

EXTREME BEGINNER

5" (12.5cm) 12g wire in your choice of metal (sterling, brass, or copper)

Wire cutters

Chain nose pliers

Masking tape

Hammer

File

Brad nail

Premade ear wires (sterling or gold-filled, depending on your metal)

Silver polishing cloth

1 Straighten the wire by holding one end in your nondominant hand. Grasp the length of that wire with your other hand, and smooth it by pulling it through your fingers from one end to the other. {a} If the kinks are stubborn, wrap the jaws of your chain nose pliers in masking tape and gently squeeze on bent areas to straighten.

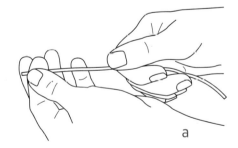

a

2 Using your wire cutters, cut the wire in half to make two 2½" (6.5cm) pieces.

3 Place the wires horizontally on your work area. Using the flat end of your ball-peen hammer, flatten one wire, moving from left to right with strong, even strokes. Metal moves in the direction it is hit, so to widen the piece, hammer with a motion that pulls the hammer toward you. Work until the earring has an appealing line, neither too narrow nor too wide. If it gets

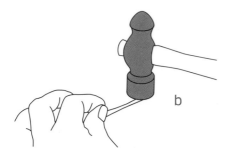

b

c

GET SITUATED

Always begin each jewelry project by sitting comfortably in your chair and squaring your hips to the bench. If you sit sideways or otherwise off-center, your technique will be compromised, and therefore your piece will be also be compromised. Resist the urge to work with your hands in your lap or braced against your knee. If you work with your limbs akimbo, you hinder your ability to do things efficiently. Always get in the practice whenever you sit at your bench of moving your chair until it's squarely facing your work area, and try your best to do all your work on or against the bench.

bent, turn up the bent edge on the table and lightly hammer the high point down. {b} Then turn the hammer over and use the ball end to create texture by hammering gently until you have a nice faceted look. Repeat with the other earring. Your arm should be somewhat sore by now. Don't worry—it's worth it!

4 Use your file to gently smooth and round both ends of each earring. Check to be sure they are the same length. If not, trim the longer one with wire cutters so they match.

5 Now use a permanent marker at the top of each earring to mark punch holes for the ear wires in the dead center of each earring, about ⅟₁₆" (1.5mm) from the top. Be sure that the hole will not be too far from the top, or the earring will not hang right. {c}

6 Use the flat end of your ball-peen hammer with a brad nail to punch the holes. File any sharp edges (burrs) on the back of the hole that were created by the nail. Buff the earrings with a polishing cloth. Insert premade ear wires to complete.

long twig earrings with beads

Love your twiggies but need some color? Follow these directions to take your basic twiggies to a new level of style.

long twig earrings with beads

MATERIALS USED FOR LONG TWIG EARRINGS PLUS

6" (15cm) of wire that fits through beads, typically 24g, 26g, or 28g

Round nose pliers

2 beads of your choosing

1 Create the Long Twig Earrings on page 24.

2 Use the marker to indicate an additional hole for the bead at the bottom of the twig ¹⁄₁₆" (1.5mm) from the edge. Punch the hole as in step 6 of the Long Twig Earrings. Buff with a polishing cloth.

3 Cut the piece of wire into two 3" (7.5cm) pieces. Take 1 piece and, using the tip of your round nose pliers, make a U shape about ½" (13mm) from the end. Now position your pliers across the U to hold the loop steady, and wrap the long end of the wire around the short piece 2 or 3 times to create a tiny coil. Snip the short end of the wire as close to the top of the coil as possible. This creates a loop onto which the bead will rest when strung. {a} String the bead onto the wire, then insert the wire through the hole in the end of the earring, and bend it down the back of the earring so the bead hangs directly beneath the earring, about ⅛" (3mm). {b}

4 Now, using your chain nose pliers or your fingernails, hold both wires at the top of the bead. Then, with your other hand, wrap the long end around the other wire twice, keeping it tight. Placing the cut at the back, snip off the excess wire as close as possible to the coil with your wire cutters. Pinch the wire end against the coil with the chain nose pliers, and straighten the bead as necessary. Repeat with the other earring, and insert the ear wires to complete.

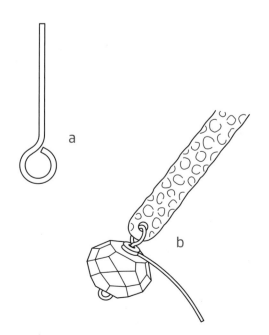

making wrapped loops

If you are using very thin wire—say, 26g or 28g—because the bead holes are very small, make wrapped loops to hold them securely. Take your wire and wrap it close to the end around the very tip of the round nose pliers to make a tiny U. With your fingers or chain nose pliers, bend the long piece of the wire up and across the short piece. Wrap it around a couple of times to form a small coil of more than 3 rows, then snip off the excess on the short end. {a–g} Press the tiny piece left from cutting to the coil with chain nose pliers. String your bead onto the loop, and finish as described in step 3 opposite.

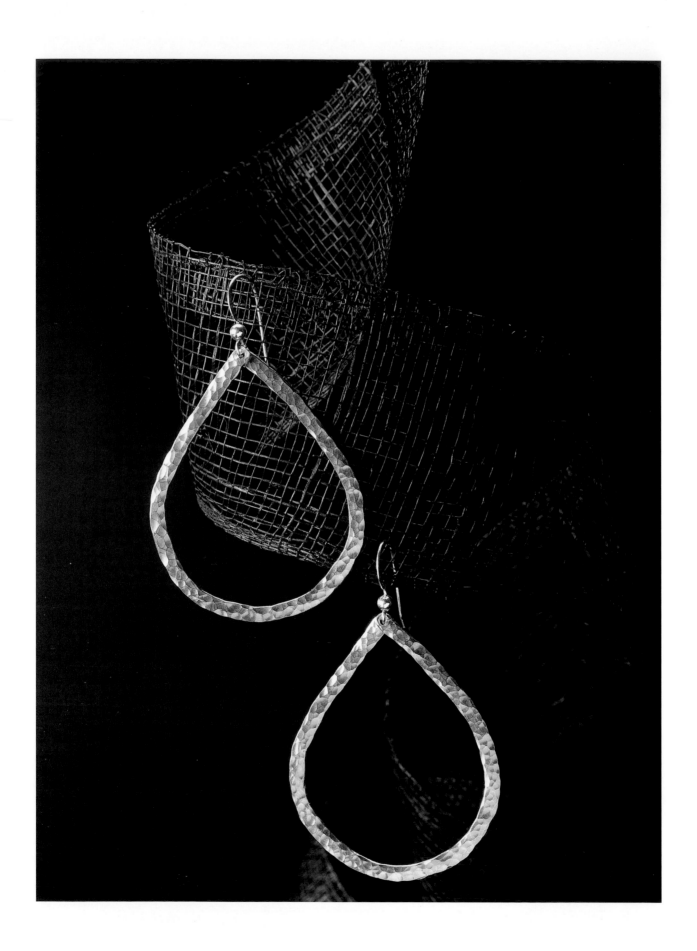

raindrop earrings

Everyone needs a good pair of hoop earrings. Clean, classic, and contemporary, hoops are the cornerstone of any jewelry wardrobe. Though not round like a traditional hoop, raindrop hoops have a gently flowing shape that flatters every face. These hoops err on the side of size and abstraction for two reasons: 1) It's easier to learn techniques on a large, free-form scale than on something tiny (and frustrating); and 2) more obviously, the size of these hoops makes them a great night-out earring. Add beads and you have a bohemian look or a dressier look, depending on the baubles you choose.

The Raindrop Earrings take the hammering and filing skills you may have learned making the Long Twig Earrings (page 24) and add forming techniques using your pliers and working from a paper template. You can use sterling, copper, or brass wire for the hoops. Size the earrings to your liking, but I recommend 1½" (3.8cm) diameter to start.

BEGINNER

2 pieces of 4½" (11.4cm) 12g wire in sterling, brass, or copper

Graph paper and pencil

Round template (optional)

Chain nose pliers

Masking tape

Ball-peen hammer

File

Brad nail

Premade ear wires of your choosing (sterling or gold-filled, depending on your metal)

Silver polishing cloth

1 To form the raindrop shape, using a round template or object like a silver dollar, draw a 1¼" (3cm) circle on a sheet of graph paper to form the bottom curve of the raindrop shape. Then, add a triangle at the top using the graph paper to make it symmetrical. Use the drawing as a guide to shape the wire.

2 Straighten both pieces of wire: To straighten, hold one end of one wire in your nondominant hand. Grasp the length of that wire with your other hand, and smooth it by pulling it through your fingers from one end to the other. If the kinks are stubborn, wrap the jaws of your chain nose pliers in masking tape and gently squeeze on bent areas to straighten.

3 File the ends of the wires until they are smooth and gently rounded.

4 Gently hold one end of your wires with your tape-wrapped chain nose pliers in your dominant hand. Now, using your other hand, begin to bend the wire by twisting your hand gently to the left (if you're right-handed), creating the start of a circle. Move in ½" (13mm) steps, curving the wire so that you have the bottom arc of a circle. Compare the shape of the wire to that of your template and adjust your curve as needed. Now, holding the right end of your wire, gently force it to the left to create the angled portion of the raindrop. Do the same with the other side, and overlap the 2

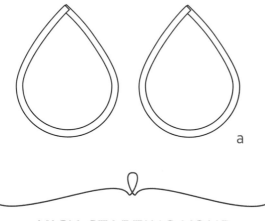

a

KICK-STARTING YOUR CREATIVITY

My students always compile a jewelry idea file to get them through those trying times when ideas have just dried up. Try starting your own file. Whenever you see an image of a piece of jewelry in a magazine or ad that has an aspect you like, tear it out and put it in a folder with pockets. While you may not love the overall design of, say, a necklace, you may like the clasp. Or you hate the piece in gold, but would like to make a version in silver. Do the same with websites and print out pictures.

Creating a file of images can help you when you need to kick-start your imagination and can also help you problem-solve a part of your design.

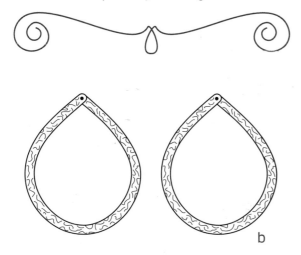

b

ends of the wire at top. Again, compare against the template and correct it as needed. When you are done, you will have an abstract raindrop shape that is open at the top. Repeat with the other earring, and compare the two. If needed, shape each earring to match the other one (rather than match the shape of your template). Don't sweat it if they are not perfect raindrop shapes—abstract is good. {a}

5 Now you are ready to hammer. Begin by opening the overlapped ends at the top a little. Hammer the earrings flat until they have a thickness and finish that you like. Check for symmetry. If the metal has become misshapen from hammering, use your chain nose pliers to correct. If the ends of the wire become stretched or otherwise out of whack, which they probably will, simply file them smooth again. Cross the ends over again and reshape until they overlap perfectly.

6 Open the crossed ends at the top a bit again, and punch holes for the ear wires in the dead center of each end of the shape. Use the flat end of your ball-peen hammer with a brad nail to punch the holes. File any burrs on the back of the hole that were created by the nail. Then, take out your premade ear wires and, using your chain nose pliers, gently open the loop at the bottom. Starting with the right side, thread both ends of the earring onto the ear wire and pinch the loop shut, thereby capturing both wires. {b}

7 Buff with a polishing cloth.

raindrop earrings
with beads

Your Raindrop hoops are beautiful in and of themselves, but if you crave color, add some beads. The number of beads is up to you: I like five at the bottom for a fringed look, but three work as well. I mixed up the shapes of the beads for interest, using both top-drilled beads and briolette beads.

raindrop earrings with beads

MATERIALS USED FOR RAINDROP EARRINGS PLUS

1' (30.5cm) of wire that fits through beads, typically 24g, 26g, or 28g

Round nose pliers

10 beads of your choosing (or however many you'd like)

1 Create the Raindrop Earrings following steps 1–7 on page 30.

2 Use a permanent marker to indicate where to punch holes for the beads at the bottom of the hoop. Use the flat end of your ball-peen hammer with a brad nail to punch the holes. File any burrs on the back of the holes that were created by the nail. {a} Finish with a polishing cloth.

3 Add beads as instructed in step 3 of the Long Twig Earrings with Beads (page 27), or, if using briolette beads like the ones shown in the photo, follow these instructions: Center your briolette bead on a 2½" (6.5cm) piece of wire, and cross the 2 ends of the wire above the bead. Bend 1 end up so it's vertical. Wrap the other end around the upward pointing wire twice with either your fingers or your pliers, making a short coil. Now, take the straight wire and thread it through the hole of the earring, bringing it around to make a loop. Wrap the remainder of the wire tightly around the existing coil and trim the excess with wire cutters. Pinch the end of the wire tightly against the coil. {b–g}

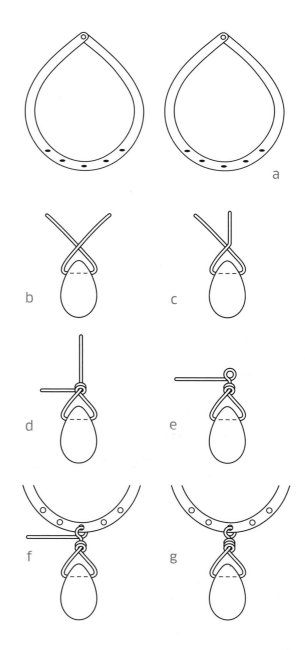

omega link chain with
handmade clasp

omega link chain with handmade clasp

Let's add a necklace (or bracelet . . . or both) to your reper-toire. This is not an abstract, handmade chain—this sleek chain lies flat and has a truly professional look. "Omega" has nothing to do with fraternities or sororities. Rather, we're talking about the Greek letter omega—you know, the one that looks like a horseshoe with legs. This simple link forms the backbone of an airy, elegant necklace that can be worn alone or with a pendant.

The possibilities are endless: I've made it 18" (45.5cm), my favorite length, but of course, it can easily be altered to be made longer or shorter. It lends itself perfectly to a match-ing bracelet of about 7" (18cm). And you can even make mini Omega Link Chains and thread them through ear wires! I've made my example in sterling silver, but any of our metals would be lovely.

What's nice about making chain is that it's a repetitive task that hones your skills. Once you've mastered creating the links, you can work in front of the TV and be done before you know it.

BEGINNER

Approximately 80" (203cm) 20g sterling silver, copper, or brass wire

Ruler

Wire cutters

Round nose pliers

Chopstick or thin pen with a diameter of about ¼" (5mm)

Chain nose pliers

File

Silver polishing cloth

1 Cut a 2" (5cm) length of wire with your wire cutters; 2" (5cm) of wire will yield a link of about 9/16" (14mm). So for the 18" (45.5cm) chain, you will need about 36 links. For a matching bracelet, you would need to make an additional 14 links. Thus, you would need an additional 28" (71cm) of wire.

2 Make a loose U shape by holding the chopstick or pen vertically in your hand while bending the wire from its center around the chopstick with your index finger and thumb.

3 Using your dominant hand, press the wire lightly against the chopstick or pen. {a}

4 With the chain nose pliers, pin the "legs" of the shape together so they are tight and straight. {b} If necessary, jiggle them up and down until they are straight. Slide the loop off the chopstick or pen. If one "leg" is longer than the other, use wire cutters to trim it.

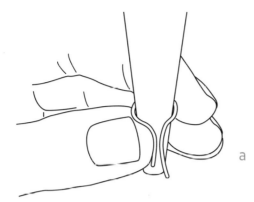

a

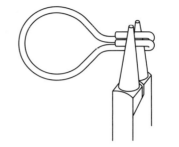

c

b

5 With your round nose pliers, curl the ends of the legs up toward the loop to make mini loops. Do not close them. If you're having trouble making them even, do 1 wire, flip the piece around, and then do the other separately. {c}

6 To assemble the chain, place the large loop of 1 link inside the double mini loops of the next link and close the mini loops with chain nose pliers. You can then fine-tune the link and loops with your pliers so they are flat and parallel.

7 For a clasp, cut another 1½" (3.8cm) length of wire and with your round nose pliers shape it into an S about ¾" (2cm) long. Loop one end of the S into the final large loop of the chain, and close it securely with chain nose pliers. Close the other end of the S partway so that it can hook onto the other loop but not come right off. File this end until smooth (see project photo).

8 Run a polishing cloth along the length of the chain to remove fingerprints.

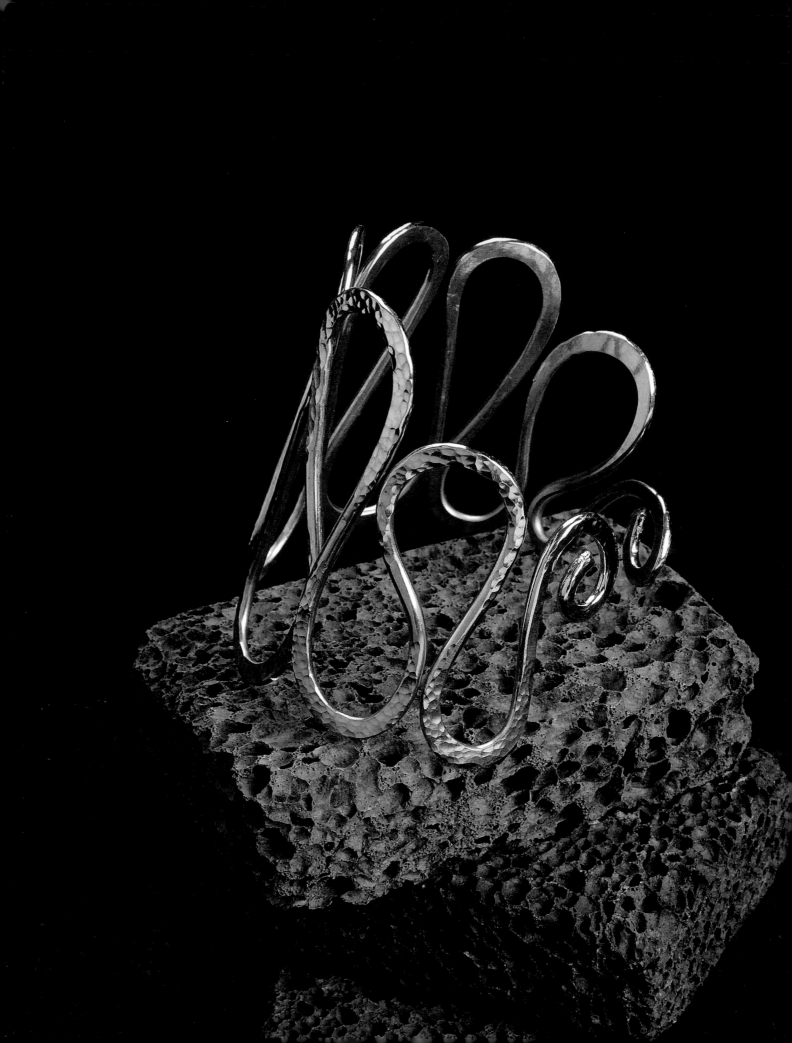

scroll cuff

Curvy is good, especially when it comes to jewelry. There is something endlessly fascinating about an abstract, shapely piece that begs to be interpreted. Wire lends itself beautifully to this task. Easy to work with, ripe for manipulation—wire is full of unexplored expression waiting to be let out. Making complicated shapes with wire is not only a good workout for the imagination, but also a good way to reinforce your shaping skills.

While the previous projects in this chapter incorporated wire wrapping, this cuff bracelet is different. You will now be using a paper drawing as a guide for your wire. You will not only bend the wire to your whim, but also stretch it with a hammer. You will learn how to shape a cuff bracelet. And when you're done, you will have a show-stopping piece that stands alone—no other jewelry necessary.

I made the one shown in copper, but sterling works just as well. It's up to you. And in keeping with my penchant for unusual uses of household items, I show how to shape the cuff using a household staple. I'll keep you in suspense while we start the project. . . .

BEGINNER

Approximately 3' (91cm) 12g wire in your choice of metal, depending on your design

Graph paper, pen and pencil, and scissors

String or thread

Wire cutters

Chain nose pliers

Round nose pliers

Masking tape

File

Hammer

Frozen juice can (frozen solid)

Paper towel or thin washcloth

Silver polishing cloth

SMALL, MEDIUM, OR LARGE?

The projects in *Chic Metal* are sized to *my* liking. Please feel free to alter any lengths, widths, beads, stones, and finishes to your liking. At first you may find it easier to stick with the measurements given. But when you become more comfortable with working with metal, you should adapt the designs to *your* liking.

1 Draw your template on graph paper with a pencil using the cuff shown for inspiration. Now, this cuff is quite wide and may overwhelm your wrist. When you draw your template, you might want to cut it out around the outline so you can better visualize the size on your wrist. A typical cuff bracelet is 6" (15cm) long, but if you have a large wrist, you will need to make it longer. Imagine it flat, and draw with that in mind. Make sure the ends of the wire are tucked

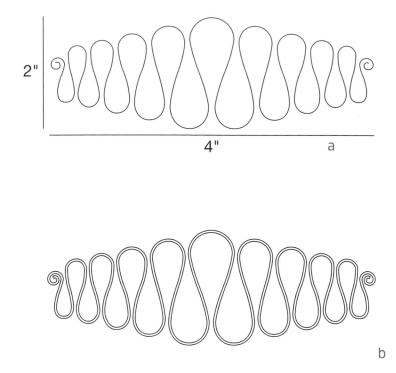

2"

4"   a

b

into the design so that they don't scratch you. You will use this design to guide your wire as you create your cuff, so draw over your pencil sketch with a pen so it doesn't smear. To determine the length of wire needed, use a piece of string and carefully move it along your drawing. Put it down against the design, pull it to the next point, and hold that point down, moving along the entire design. If it helps, tape the string down at different points so that your measurement is accurate. Mark your string where the design ends. Be sure to add about 2" (5cm) to be safe, as the wire we are using is thicker than the string. You can always shorten it, but you can't make it longer! {a}

2 Cut the wire to length and file the ends smooth. Wrap your round nose and chain nose pliers in masking tape. Now, carefully mold the wire into the shape of your design using your drawing to guide you (for more on working with a template, see step 4 of the Raindrop Earrings, page 30). {b} This may take some doing, so go slow—and, if necessary to correct the shape, straighten the wire as you go along by gently easing the kinks with your chain nose pliers. Trim the excess wire at the end.

3 When you are happy with your design, you are ready to hammer. Rather than flattening the whole thing, we're just hammering certain areas so that the cuff has some dimension. I prefer to hammer the broad curves. Flatten

DON'T SCRAP YOUR SCRAPS

Always save your leftover bits of metal from cutting wire or sheet to size, no matter how insignificant they may seem to you. Sometimes you may find yourself needing a tiny piece for a project, and you don't want to cut it from a larger sheet or length of wire. Scrap sterling silver can be sold. You can also do this with brass or copper, although it's not really worth it unless you have pounds of it lying around. Separate your scraps by type of metal and keep them in small-lidded plastic containers for future use.

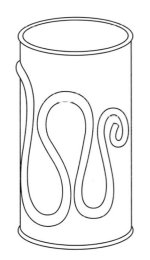

C

the surfaces you want with the flat side of your hammer. Move your hammer with a down-and-out motion so you really pull the metal and add width to the wire. Then texture the areas you want with the ball end of your hammer.

TIP If you're having trouble hammering on a wood surface, consider using an old claw hammer as a small anvil. If you lay it on its side flat on your bench, you'll see the head makes a nice little anvil on which to work.

4 Lay the frozen juice can down on your bench, and place the middle of the cuff on the can. Using your bare hands, bend the metal down around the can. {C} You may want to wrap it in a paper towel or a thin washcloth so that your hands don't freeze. Wrap as far as

you can until the metal hits the bench. Now, flip the whole thing over—can and metal. Using the flat side of your hammer, very carefully hammer one end toward the can, shaping it into a half circle. Again, the metal will move in response to where the hammer hits, so try to *pull* the end toward the other with even strokes of your hammer. Repeat on the other side. Try on the cuff, and adjust if necessary. Continue until you are satisfied with the fit. You can always press the cuff into shape with your hands at this point and, indeed, it will conform to your wrist as you wear it, sometimes becoming surprisingly out of whack in the process!

5 Buff with a polishing cloth.

two

the saw, drill, and dremel

By now you have tested the waters of making metal jewelry. You have cut, hammered, filed, and formed. You have, perhaps, struggled but persevered to complete some pretty cool projects. Armed with your newfound skills and confidence, you are ready to tackle something new! I now present to you the saw, the drill, and the dremel.

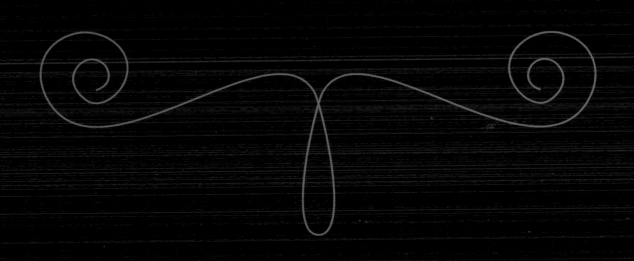

The Saw

I would be remiss as a teacher and jeweler if I did not advise you from the outset that sawing is one of the more difficult techniques to master and with which to feel comfortable. Why do I mention this? Although I have stressed the importance of patience in jewelry making, sawing will test you. It's delicate, it's difficult if you haven't done it before, and it can be vexing. This is why I teach sawing to my students early on: Once mastered, it paves the way for more complex skill building and opens up infinite possibilities in jewelry making.

A jewelers' saw is quite like a regular saw, save for its size and the delicacy of its blade. It has a flexible, sliding frame and tiny blades that will test your vision. (Buy some magnifiers if necessary—they may help later, too.) But let's not belabor this; let's just begin.

Unscrew the thumbscrew at the bottom of your saw just next to the handle. Take a blade out of the package. It is intimidatingly small, but don't dismay. Hold it up vertically in front of you—with a light source behind it, ideally—and look at its teeth. Flip the blade until the teeth point down toward the saw handle. It should look like half of a Christmas tree.

Now, keeping the blade in this position, insert one end between the saw frame and small metal block by the thumbscrew you opened near the handle. The teeth should point out, not toward the frame. You can't saw if they face in! Tighten it down. Next, see where the end of the blade is in relation to the end of the saw frame. It should hit the clamp at about the middle. If not, undo the bolt at the top of the saw frame and adjust it in or out until perfect. Be sure to tighten each thumbscrew securely. Open the back thumbscrew and insert the blade.

The most crucial aspect to successful sawing is to make sure the blade is super tight. Here's my secret to doing this: With the blade firmly held in the bolt near the handle, press the end of the saw handle against your hip bone or stomach, and press the other end against the edge of your bench. This flexes the frame a little and allows you to tighten the thumbscrew. When the tension is released, the blade will be taut, almost immovable. Pluck it gently like a guitar string. It should "ping." If it doesn't, it's not taut enough; open one end and repeat.

You are now ready to begin. Although some professional jewelers choose not to lubricate their blades, I like to, using natural or synthetic beeswax, soap, or a candle. Whichever you choose, run it up the blade once or twice.

Sawing Sheet Metal

The proper position for sawing anything metal is to move the saw *vertically* up and down the piece of metal—yes, vertically. We are not sawing a 2 x 4.

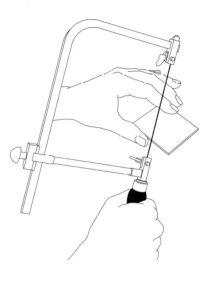

The best way to hold a saw frame is loosely. Hold the handle in your hand and stabilize it with your index finger and thumb. Resist the urge to grip it tight like a hammer. Instead, keep your hand and forearm relaxed. Practice on a piece of scrap metal. Holding the metal so that the edge is very slightly off your bench, gently take a couple of downward strokes at about a 45-degree angle at the overhanging edge where you want to saw so you have a little groove in which to work. Now, gently, while moving your saw up and down, rotate your hand holding the saw upward to a position that's vertical. Continue to gently move your saw up and down, making a thin cut, never forcing the blade forward, but rather letting it do its work while you guide it with your hand. You are now on a journey, sometimes vexing, sometimes exhilarating. I recommend practicing quite a bit on scrap metal sheet before beginning a project.

You will break a blade. You will break five. You may break five hundred. No matter—this is no reflection of your ability to do metal jewelry. I would say ninety percent of the time, blade breaking is a result of not having the blade taut enough. Check the blade, tighten if necessary, relax your grip, and start again. Just keep at it.

After practicing a bit, you may now be bored of going in a straight line, and indeed you will need to saw a curve at some point. Here's how: When you are ready to make a curve, keep moving your saw up and down, as before, without pushing forward, and slowly move the metal in the direction you want. Always move the metal—not your saw, because you may break the blade by wrenching it around while it's in the metal. Even in a very tight turn, do the same technique as above: Move the saw up and down without trying to go forward. Just do the motion, and gently turn the metal until it is positioned where you want it.

Practice this. Practice it again. Take a candy bar break—you will want some energy. Then practice some more.

Sawing Wire

This time, I left the easiest task for last. You will find sawing wire completely and rewardingly simple after hacking away at sheet metal. Here's how: Simply hold your wire against the edge of your bench and gently saw, as above, this time angling your saw forward at a 45-degree angle. Some people just saw wire vertically, but I think the angle facilitates things. Practice this, too, until you can saw the wire straight through.

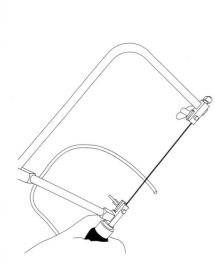

Here are some tips on sawing both sheet metal and wire, culled from years of frustration and triumph:

1 Let the tool do the work. As I mentioned in the first chapter, never force a tool. Hold the saw loosely in your hand. Once you loosen what will inevitably be a viselike grip, things will be much easier because you will be letting the saw do its thing without you. (And you'll save yourself from muscular exhaustion, too.)

2 Think of making the sawing motion from your shoulder, not from your wrist. Doing this will make the blade move up and down on a straight axis, not all over the place as your wrist does. Again, it's less tiring.

3 Whenever you saw, make a concerted effort to square your hips to your bench so that you are working directly in front of you, which you should be used to doing by now.

4 Always mark where you are going to saw with a permanent marker or by scratching a light mark in the metal with the scribe you made from a coat hanger.

5 Always cut just *outside* of your line. You can always file off excess, but you can't add more.

6 If you break a saw blade in the middle of sawing a line, insert a new one, and begin again by very lightly sawing through the cut you have just made until you get to the end where the blade broke. Don't try to just force the blade through the cut—it'll just break again!

7 Most importantly, resist the urge to go fast. Sawing can take time, and it can be a bore. However, you will break fewer blades and, ultimately, get to the finish line faster if you take your time.

The Dremel
Drilling

Compared with the saw, the drill is your friend. Drilling metal is a relatively basic jewelry-making technique. Thank goodness, you say—enough with breaking saw blades already. Don't relax just yet, though. Although drilling is most often used to simply make a hole, it's a key component in a different method of sawing called piercing, in which you cut out a design within your piece of metal. It's similar to piercing an ear (minus the pain and rubbing alcohol). Learning how to pierce metal opens up your jewelry-making options greatly by allowing you to add intricacy to your designs.

You will use a drill bit in your Dremel instead of hammering with a brad nail for all drilling purposes in the forthcoming projects. A Dremel is a basic high-speed rotary tool. It resembles an electric toothbrush with a small motor and a chuck at the end that opens and closes to accommodate different accessories mounted to steel sticks (mandrels). You can use a Dremel for a plethora of household tasks, and perhaps you have already done so. I like the 300 Series, which can be had for about $50 at any good hardware store. Whichever model you choose, make sure it has an adjustable speed control and a Jacobs® chuck.

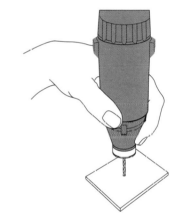

Always wear goggles when doing anything with your Dremel. We're talking about protecting your eyesight here. Get in the habit of putting your goggles on the moment you need to use the Dremel—no exceptions.

The Dremel and other rotary tools are designed to be held in a couple of ways. For most jewelry work, hold the Dremel as you would a pen. Writing is one of the most complicated finemotor tasks we do, so it makes a great analogy for the grip needed when finishing with a Dremel. It will feel uncomfortable at first, but stick with it. Because jewelry making is precise and tiny in a way that cleaning grout is not, you need to have a lot of control.

Insert the drill bit in the chuck and tighten carefully. I recommend that you check to see whether the drill bit is positioned exactly in the chuck before you begin. Simply run the Dremel while holding it in your hand and check that the drill is spinning vertically and not wobbling around, which

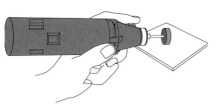

can be dangerous. Always take a moment to make a little divot in your metal to guide the drill bit. You can simply use a center punch or one of the scribes you made, and tap it with a hammer where you wish to drill. The divot does not need to be deep at all—just deep enough to anchor the drill bit so it has a place to start and doesn't skitter all over the metal, causing scratching and tears.

Whenever possible, use the Dremel (for drilling and for polishing) while your hand is braced on or against the bench. With the other hand, hold your piece and brace on or against the bench, too. You will have much less control if you hold the Dremel and your piece up in the air. Get used to always bracing both hands on the bench.

Now, practice on a piece of scrap metal. Make a divot, turn on your Dremel and run it at a low speed, and turn it upside down until it's vertical to your metal. Slowly push the drill bit into the metal until it's drilled all the way through. Resist the urge to force the drill into the metal: Again, let the tool do the work.

Here are a couple of tips that will make your drilling life easier:

1 If you are repeatedly drilling a thick piece of metal, you may find that the piece heats up until it's difficult to touch. In this case, have a bowl of water handy and just dip the piece in whenever you need to. The water will not affect the process.

2 You can facilitate drilling in the same way as sawing by lubricating the drill. There are commercial products you can buy, like Bur Life, but liquid dish soap or a candle work just fine, too.

Polishing

In addition to using the Dremel to drill, you will use it to smooth and polish your pieces. A Dremel can come with a kit of bewildering attachments. Ignore all of those for now except for a rubber polishing wheel and any felt or muslin wheels. If the Dremel does not include polishing wheels, you can get them separately at jewelry supply stores and many hardware stores.

The order of polishing is rough to smooth. You can tell the roughness, or aggressiveness, of each wheel by how it feels. Wheels that remove metal (and therefore scratches) feel rougher to the touch; wheels that polish feel smoother and softer when pressed. For the projects in *Chic*

Metal, always begin with a rubber wheel and finish with a felt or muslin wheel coated with the polishing compounds tripoli or rouge, which are used *only* with a felt or cloth buff.

Always begin by polishing out scratches with a rubber wheel inserted in the Dremel. Run the Dremel for a moment to make sure the wheel spins perfectly straight and doesn't wobble. Sometimes the mandrel of the wheel may become imperceptibly bent and throw the wheel off center. In addition to causing unnecessary friction that needs to be controlled by gripping the Dremel hard and overtaxing your hand, it can be dangerous because it can force the metal out of your hand. Use a low speed and simply rub the wheel back and forth over the area you wish to smooth. I recommend that you think of your Dremel as a giant eraser. When you are removing scratches and polishing, you are deleting unwanted marks, which include removing a dull surface from your metal as a final step. Simply think of it as erasing the defects in the metal, with a smooth back-and-forth motion.

When you are satisfied, you are ready for tripoli. Insert a felt or cloth buff in the chuck and tighten. This will be your tripoli buff, and it is to be used with tripoli only. Be sure to use two different buffs with tripoli and rouge, as mixing the tripoli with the rouge will defeat the purpose of the latter. I like to use a permanent marker to color the mandrel of the tripoli buff black so I can tell the difference between the two. When you have checked the wheel's position, as before, while running the Dremel, press it gently into the bar of tripoli and "charge" the buff until it has a thin coat. Don't go nuts here: Tripoli is very greasy and will gunk up your piece even under the best of circumstances. More will make it even worse. Polish the piece, "recharging" the wheel as necessary. This is an intuitive step: I really can't explain when the wheel should be recharged, but you will see as you go along. Now, wash the piece well with soap and water, using a tiny bit of ammonia if the grease is really stubborn, and dry it.

Then you will give it a final polish with a different soft buff, one coated with rouge. As with the tripoli, charge the new buff with rouge and polish until bright and shiny. Wash your piece well with soap and water and pat dry with a paper towel. Try not to aggressively rub the piece dry at this point: After all, a paper towel is made of wood, which can leave scratches in the metal you have just worked so hard to polish.

A couple of polishing tips are as follows:

1 While I usually stress "letting the tool do the work," with the case of polishing with tripoli and rouge, a little pressure can help a lot. Keep a bowl of water handy in case the piece should heat up while polishing. Simply dunk it in, dry it, and begin again.

2 Using a felt wheel, rather than a muslin buff, with tripoli makes the tripoli more aggressive and will remove tiny scratches faster than a buff alone. A caveat, however—when polishing a wide, flat surface, it is easy to create wavelike dips in the metal by applying pressure with the felt buff in some areas more than others. So use a muslin buff instead when polishing wide, flat surfaces.

3 If you find you are leaving quite a few deep scratches in your projects, consider getting a few rubber wheels of different hardnesses. For stubborn marks, I like to use a white rubber wheel, followed by a black one, and then the blue. Again, you can see how aggressive a wheel is by pressing it. Ones that will take out a lot of scratches feel rough, like pumice stone. Smooth ones that "give" when you press them will polish.

4 Use a smooth, slow back-and-forth motion with any polishing wheel. Don't wiggle your hand quickly all over the piece: It's not only inefficient but also dangerous if you're not being careful to hold the piece firmly.

hammered disc earrings

hammered disc earrings

These disc earrings seem simple. So simple, in fact, that they're usually taken for granted in the jewelry world. Nevertheless, they are my favorites, as well as one of my best-sellers of all time. For me, the circle is the most satisfying of all geometric shapes. These have some sparkle, and—as with almost all of the jewelry I favor—are bold and beautiful. At 1½" (3.8cm) in diameter, they are big, but not overwhelmingly so. (Of course, as with any project in this book, alter the size to suit your taste.) They go perfectly with a chic, black ensemble. I love them in sterling silver or brass. I love them with a T-shirt. I love them with a Pucci-esque dress. Heck, I just love them! (Can you tell?) One caveat—they may look easy to make, but they require precision, even more precision than the wire jewelry you've already done.

1 Using a template (page 152) or a round object about the size of a silver dollar, draw two 1½" (3.8cm) circles on paper. Carefully cut them out. These are your templates that will be glued to your metal to guide sawing the shapes.

2 Thoroughly wash your metal sheet with the toothbrush, soap, and water. Dry thoroughly. Coat the circles with the glue stick and apply them to your sheet next to each other. Be sure that each circle is completely attached to your metal sheet, with no edges curling up. Let them dry for 5 minutes.

3 Prepare your saw as described on page 44, and drag the blade across the beeswax, soap, or candle to lubricate it. Take a deep breath and begin sawing just outside the line of your circle. Again, move the metal slowly and carefully as you go around the curves. Repeat with the other earring.

4 Peel off your paper templates and clean the remaining glue off the metal. Now use your file to remove any bumps on the edges or any irregular areas. Check your piece against a template. It should be as circular and perfect

as possible. This may take a little time—stick with it.

5 Now, using the ball end of your hammer, evenly hammer the surface of each earring. Be sure your hammer strokes overlap one another so that the entire surface is covered with little marks. You do not want "blank" areas between the hammer marks—this looks unprofessional. Keep at it. The edges will start to curl up. I think this "potato chip" look is nice, as it catches the light better than a flat sheet. If you prefer a flat look, place the earring on your bench or cutting board, hammered side down, and gently flatten it with the flat side of your hammer. Gently file the edges if the metal has become misshapen.

6 Now use a permanent marker at the top of each earring to mark holes for ear wires in the dead center of each earring, and drill the holes using the Dremel and the drill bit.

7 Go around the edges of the earrings with a rubber wheel in the Dremel until smooth. Insert your tripoli buff in the Dremel and polish both the edges and surface of each earring. You can polish the back too, if you're inclined to do so. Wash them well with soap and water, then dry and polish them with the rouge buff and rouge. Wash again, pat dry, and then insert the ear wires.

HAMMER HELPER

You may find that the finish on your hammer starts to dull or becomes scratched from repeated use. The easiest way to return it to its original luster is to use simple wet/dry sandpaper from the hardware store. Start with a rough sheet like 220 grit. Cut it into a small, manageable piece, and sand the face of your hammer in a circular motion. When it is smooth, continue sanding with 300-grit sandpaper. Then, use finer grits in order of 400, 500, and 600. You're done when it looks nice and shiny again.

oval disc earrings with dangles

An oval is a universally flattering earring shape. It can lengthen a round face, it can highlight a beautiful neck, and it can add symmetry and balance. I think of it as a "calm" shape—easy to grasp, soothing, even. These oval earrings are adorned with mini ovals and circles for a dynamic and fluttery feel. I like to use sterling silver or brass—you can even mix up the two, making the disc portion in sterling and the dangles in brass, for example.

This project reinforces the sawing skills you had begun to master with the Hammered Discs (page 51). We won't hammer in this one—you need a break, after all!—but you will use that time for sawing on a much smaller scale. Remember, in jewelry making, working big is easier than working little. You've done big—now let's tackle tiny. There's another trick in this project as well: You'll learn how to saw two of the same pieces at once. And it will introduce you to a type of "cold connection" (i.e., connecting pieces without solder)— jump rings. You'll also learn the right way to give a matte finish to a large area. Finally, I'll show you how to increase the jingle factor of these earrings by adding beads.

CONFIDENT BEGINNER

1" x 2½" (2.5cm x 6.5cm) sheet 24g sterling silver or brass (a piece of each metal if using both)

Graph paper, pencil, and scissors

Glue stick

Toothbrush

Ruler

Saw frame and blades

Beeswax, soap, or candle

File

Center punch and hammer

Drill bit

Dremel with blue rubber wheel and tripoli buff

Tripoli

Small jump rings

Premade ear wires of your choosing (sterling or gold-filled, depending on your metal)

Scotch-Brite pad

Beads (optional)

Cut Out the Shapes

1 Using a template (page 152), draw two ¾" x ⅝" tall (2cm x 16mm) ovals on paper. If you are not using templates, here's how to make a nice, symmetrical oval using the "snowflake" method (this technique is great for any shape that requires symmetry). Fold a piece of graph paper in half. Now draw half of the oval at the fold, ¾" (2cm) tall but only about ⅓" (8mm) wide. Carefully cut out and open. You will have a nice, even oval. {a}

2 Lubricate your saw blade with beeswax, soap, or a candle. Measure your metal, mark it at the middle, and saw it in half.

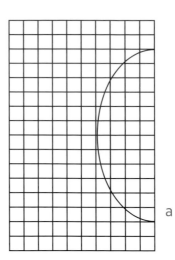

a

3 Wash your metal with a toothbrush, soap, and water, and then dry with a paper towel. Apply a thick layer of the glue stick to one half of the metal sheet, press the other half on top of it, and place a heavy book or pot on top of them. Let dry for 5 minutes. Now glue your template onto the top sheet. Let dry for 5 minutes. Saw out the oval, being sure to saw just outside your template. File the edges smooth. Pry apart the 2 sheets of metal and marvel at how quick it is to saw 2 shapes with this method!

4 Now you will need to make 2 each of the round and oval dangle templates. I like to use 2 ovals and 2 circles per earring—1 oval at the top and 1 at the bottom, flanked by 2 circles. Even though you'll be making 4 ovals and 4 circles, you'll only have to saw *twice* because we're going to double up the sheets again.

5 Again, using the "snowflake" method, create two ¼" tall x ³⁄₁₆" wide (6mm x 4mm) ovals. Cut out carefully.

6 Lubricate your saw blade with beeswax, soap, or candle and saw the remaining half of the metal sheet in half. Thoroughly scrub the sheets with toothbrush, soap, and water, and then dry. Apply a thick layer of the glue stick to 1 sheet, press the other sheet on top of it, and place a heavy book or pot on top of them. Let dry for 5 minutes.

7 Apply the oval paper templates, as in step 3, keeping them close together to minimize waste. Saw out the shapes. Again, move the metal slowly and carefully as you go around the curves. This will be tough because the ovals are tiny. Take your time. If you mess up, make another. Believe it or not, it's faster in the end to just start over than to try to correct mistakes. Cut out both ovals.

8 Leaving the ovals glued together, file the edges of each as perfect as possible. Pry apart the sheets.

9 Repeat this process to make four ¼" (6mm) circles. Now smooth the entire oval and circle edges with your Dremel and rubber wheel. Polish each with your tripoli buff and tripoli. Now, it may seem counterproductive to shine up a piece of metal to which you are going to give a matte finish, but all the marks need to be

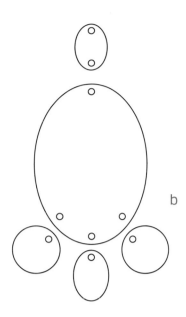

b

c

removed, or the matte finish will not look intentional—it will just look sloppy and scratched. Trust me. Wash well and pat dry.

10 Using a permanent marker and a ruler, find the middle point at the bottom of your large oval. Mark it, and then make 2 evenly spaced marks on each side. These marks are where you will drill. Make a mark near the top of each small oval and circle and an additional mark near the bottom of one of the small ovals. Make a divot on each mark with your center punch. Insert your drill bit in the Dremel and drill the holes. If there are burrs, run a rubber wheel over them until smooth. {b}

11 Now you are ready to matte. Using a Scotch-Brite pad, methodically scrub each piece of metal *in one direction* only. This is the oft-ignored trick to giving a professional matte finish. Scrub both sides of each piece.

Assemble the Earrings

12 Always set out the pieces to be assembled in the order in which they go together so that you can be methodical and orderly. Take out your jump rings. Hold one side of the jump ring seam-side up in your pliers. Then grasp the other side with pliers or your fingernails, and twist one half toward the back to open it slightly. (Do not expand the ring side to side; that will warp the circle and it won't close properly.) Slip the opened ring first through the central dangle and then through the large oval, and close by pushing the jump ring edges back together so no gap remains. Make sure it's tight. Now do the same with the other dangles, working outward.

13 Insert ear wires as shown in previous projects. Now, inspect the earrings for marks made while assembling, and gently use the Scotch-Brite pad to remove them. It's nice to finish the ear wire in the same manner. You have now conquered sawing the small!

TIP For a variation, you can use as many ovals, circles, or squiggles as you like. You can add beads as well. Just assemble the earrings, and attach the beads as shown in the Long Twig Earrings with Beads (page 27).

mixed-metal chain
with pendant

A simple, beautiful handmade chain always looks great, and it is a true departure from mass-market and fine jewelry chains. I like one with a slightly chunky look, adorned with simple, dramatic pendants. This is the simplest of chains—wire rings linked together for an airy look. The directions are for an 18" (45.5cm) chain, but altering the length is easy: just use more or fewer jump rings. I've made it with mixed sterling and brass wire for a two-tone look. This way, it goes with both white metal jewelry and gold jewelry. It is also great for those days when you just can't make up your mind.

This project teaches you to make perfect links using the most mundane of household objects. The pendants are a take on earrings from chapter 1, but with a little more precision. Here you'll learn how to make wire rings all the same size, knowledge you can later use when you need jump rings and can't get to a store.

ADVANCED BEGINNER

40" (101.5cm) 16g brass wire (approximate measurement—depends on size of pen)

40" (101.5cm) 14g sterling silver wire (approximate measurement—depends on size of pen)

File

Round nose pliers

Plastic pen with a diameter of about 5⁄16" (8mm) (will yield 1⁄2" [13mm] links)

Thin chopstick or pen with a diameter of about 3⁄16" (4mm) (will yield 1⁄4" [6mm] links)

Saw frame and blades

Beeswax, soap, or candle

3" (7.5cm) 16g sterling silver wire for clasp

7" (18cm) 12g sterling silver wire for pendants

10" (25.5cm) 12g brass wire for pendants

Standard 6-ounce (177ml) nail polish remover bottle or 1-liter soda bottle with top (used to form links)

Hammer

File

Center punch

Drill bit

Dremel with blue rubber wheel, tripoli buff, and rouge buff

Tripoli

Rouge

Silver polishing cloth

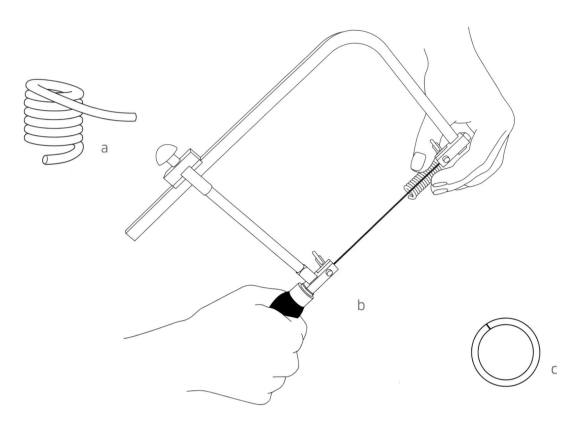

Make the Links

1 Uncoil your 16g brass wire. Use the brass wire before the sterling since it's not as expensive, and any boo-boos and mistakes will hurt less.

2 Hold the pen in your nondominant hand. With your other hand, press the end of the wire tightly against the pen, and then begin to wrap it tightly around the pen. It will start to look like a coil. Be sure to use strong, even pressure so that the coil is very consistent. Do this until you have a 1" (2.5cm) coil to start. Slide the coil off the pen and use wire cutters to nip off the rest of the wire. {a}

3 Insert a blade in your saw frame and lube it with beeswax, soap, or a candle. Now, hold the coil on each side with your index finger and thumb. Angle it along the edge of your bench at about a 45-degree angle with your fingers pointing toward you. Place your saw next to the wire end, and carefully begin sawing at the bottom of the coil. Saw through the coil so that, with each layer of wire, a symmetrical circle is formed and falls away. {b} You will now have perfect links measuring about 5/16" (8mm), as well as a little piece leftover. Set the links aside.

4 Use chain nose pliers to open 1 ring from front to back (see illustration {c} on page 57). Inspect the edges. Are they perfectly smooth and aligned? If not, carefully file until they are. Close the ring and check the seam by holding it up to the light. It should be nice and snug, with no gap—meaning almost no light coming through. {c}

5 Open another link, check it, fix it, and now thread one end through the previous link. Close it, and you'll begin to see the chain forming. Now take them apart again. Go back and make more, using the rest of your wire, until you

GET A LITTLE SHUT-EYE

My students always look at me strangely the first time they see me take one of their pieces, hold it up in front of me, and shut one eye to look at it. But shutting one eye is one the best ways to examine a piece and check for accuracy. Simply hold up your piece and without thinking, close one of your eyes. Just do what comes naturally. Your brain will automatically shut the less dominant eye. Get in the habit of doing this when examining a piece for even edges, polished surface, or really, anything else for that matter. After a couple of goes, it will become second nature and your pieces will be better for getting some shut-eye.

have 31 brass links. You will use 26 of them for the chain, and 5 to attach the pendants.

6 Repeat steps 1–5 with the sterling wire. Continue until you have made 25 sterling links. These links should measure ⁹⁄₁₆" (14.3mm).

Assemble the Chain

7 Open a link, check it to make sure the edges are flush, fix them with a file if necessary, and now thread one end through the next link. Alternate the sterling and brass links until your chain is complete.

8 Using the 3" (7.5cm) piece of wire, form a clasp as described in the Omega Link Chain in step 7 on page 37. Put the whole necklace together and admire it.

Make the Pendants

9 Since "round" is the theme here, it follows to make some round pendants. I like a diameter of about 1" (2.5cm) and have found that the top of a standard bottle of nail polish remover or a 1-liter soda bottle top makes for a perfect mandrel. Take out your 12g wires and file 1 edge straight. Using the same method as on the pen in step 2, make 3 rings with the sterling wire and 2 rings with the brass wire on the nail polish remover cap.

10 Unlike the thinner wire you are accustomed to using, thicker wire like this may spring apart and otherwise be unruly. Check the edges for precision, and close each link. To keep the edges together, you will need to build up tension in the metal so that the edges will spring together and stay put. Very gently, open the ends of the link about ⅛" (3mm). Now move the ends together, crossing one end over the other; now cross them on the other side, making a side-by-side motion with your hands. Try closing the link. It should spring into shape. If not, repeat this step. You can also open the link from front to back a few times, again crossing

one end on top of the other. The ends should now line up perfectly.

11 Using the flat portion of your hammer, judiciously flatten each circle into a nice, smooth shape. This is the same technique as the one you may have learned in making the Raindrop Earrings in chapter 1 (page 30). Do this carefully: You don't want to alter the shape of the circle if you can help it. Texture with the ball side of the hammer if you wish—again, do so carefully.

12 This may have warped the ends of the wire so that they do not meet as well, but this is not a big deal unless they are truly off. If they are, open the link, file the edges, and build up tension again as in step 10 so they meet. Repeat this process with the other 4 links.

TIP The size of your circles may vary depending on how much stretching of the metal occurred while forming. And sterling will always stretch a bit more than brass. Hopefully, you will see the beauty of these discrepancies, but if not, get out your math hat and figure out how much smaller you should make the sterling circles.

13 Mark a hole with a permanent marker or scribe close to the edge on each pendant link. Make a divot with your center punch, and drill the holes using your Dremel and drill bit to accommodate 16g wire. Polish the links with a rubber wheel and then your tripoli buff and tripoli. Wash the pieces well and dry. Follow with rouge, wash well, and gently pat dry with a paper towel.

Attach the Pendants

14 Lay out the chain in a straight line. The easiest way to find the center is to count the sterling rings and find the middle one. Set down 1 of the brass pendants in front of the center link in the chain. Set down a sterling pendant about 2 sterling rings away on each side of the central pendant. Set down the remaining 2 brass pendants the same distance from the outer ones. {e}

15 You will use 5 of your remaining brass links as jump rings to attach the pendants. Thread 1 through the central pendant. Insert the ring in the appropriate chain link and close. Repeat with the other 4 pendants.

16 Buff with a polishing cloth to remove any fingerprints if necessary.

make it a bracelet

To make a matching bracelet, just shorten the chain to fit your wrist. The bracelet pictured here is 6½" (16.5cm) long and contains 16 sterling ¼" (6mm) links and 7 brass ½" (13mm) links. I made this one without the pendants, but they'd be a nice addition here, too.

cuff bracelet

One of my favorite pieces of jewelry is a simple, stunning cuff bracelet. It's all you need to complete an outfit. This version, though a substantial 2½" (6.5cm) wide, is lightweight and easy to wear... and you can tailor the width to suit your style. Instead of the usual hammered finish, this bracelet is textured with simple etching using the scribe you have made with a coat hanger (see Bench Basics, page 10). The abstract lines add interest and sparkle. I made my cuff in brass, but this style lends itself to all metals. You'll have to saw again for this project, and this time in a straight line (eek!), but we're working with thin metal, which will make your life easier.

ADVANCED BEGINNER

24g sheet of sterling silver or brass, at least 2½" x 6" (6.5cm x 15cm)

Ruler

Permanent marker or scribe

Saw frame and blades

Beeswax, soap, or candle

File

220-grit sandpaper

Hammer

Frozen juice can (frozen solid)

Paper towel or thin washcloth

Dremel with blue rubber wheel, tripoli buff, and rouge buff

Tripoli

Rouge

Scotch-Brite pad (if creating a matte finish)

Cut the Sheet

1 If you are working with a sheet larger than 2½" x 6" (6.5cm x 15cm), you will need to first saw it to this measurement. (If your sheet is ready to go, skip to step 3.) Using your ruler, measure 2½" (6.5cm) from one edge of your metal. Mark it, and then do the same a couple of times across to line up the dots. Connect the dots with a permanent marker or gently scratch with your scribe.

2 Lubricate your saw blade with beeswax, soap, or a candle, and saw the metal along the line you've just created, remembering to cut just outside of your line.

NOTE This is somewhat difficult. You may peter out halfway through; you may go all over the place with your saw. Be patient and make sure you're sawing well clear of your line in case you start to cut into it. Use your file to clean up the edge you just sawed, or hold the edge down on sandpaper and push forward and backward.

3 Using a permanent marker, draw quarter circles at each corner of the sheet. These will guide you in sawing off the corners so that

a

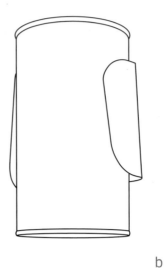

b

they won't cut you when you wear it. Saw the quarter circles out and file them round and smooth. {a}

4 To texture the cuff like the one shown, use your scribe to scratch a bunch of deep lines into the sheet. I like irregular crisscross marks in groups, some deeper and wider than others. Continue until you're happy with the results.

Shape the Cuff

5 Lay the frozen juice can down on your bench, and place the middle of the cuff on the can. Using your bare hands, bend the metal down around the can. You may want to wrap it in a paper towel or a dishcloth so your hands don't freeze. Go as far as you can go until the metal hits the bench. Now flip the whole thing over—can and metal. Using the flat side of your hammer, very carefully hammer one end toward the can, shaping it into a half circle. Repeat on the other end. {b}

6 At this point, your cuff will undoubtedly be too big. Continue forming it with just your hands, if possible, or, if necessary, with the hammer. Working both sides at the same time, push the edges of the cuff together until you have a good fit for your wrist. The cuff will inevitably bend while you wear it to conform to your wrist, so don't worry too much about warping it now.

7 Use your Dremel with a rubber wheel to smooth the edges of the cuff. Now use your tripoli buff and tripoli on the surface. This will shine up the places on the cuff without scratches, leaving the scratches rough and a little darker. You can even use a permanent marker over the scratched areas and then polish it a bit—this gives it a patina and adds depth. Wash the cuff with soap and water, and wear it well. If you prefer a matte finish, use a Scotch-Brite pad and remember, methodically scrub the cuff *in one direction* only.

charm bracelet

charm bracelet

INTERMEDIATE

20g sheet of sterling or your choice of metal, at least 3" x 3" (7.5cm x 7.5cm)

5" (12.5cm) 20g wire

7"–7½" (18cm–19cm) thick premade round wire curb chain that will accommodate the jump rings used to attach the charms (to determine the length of chain needed, measure wrist first)

Graph paper, pencil, and scissors

Glue stick

Beeswax, soap or candle

Saw frame and blades

File

Center punch and hammer

Drill bit

Dremel with blue rubber wheel, tripoli buff, and rouge buff

Tripoli

Rouge

Chain nose pliers

Premade jump rings in a matching metal that fit into your chain

Scotch-Brite pad (if creating a matte finish)

A charm bracelet is a great way to add a little cuteness and fun to your jewelry wardrobe. What I appreciate most about a charm bracelet—especially one that is chunky and makes a statement—is that it lends itself perfectly to the task of customization. A charm bracelet can tell a story about you—the shapes you like, the things you like, whether you're nostalgic or you live in the present, whether you are a romantic or you are a realist. I favor iconic shapes, and the images I chose for this bracelet reflect this. Rather than creating a narrative, I made a set of charms out of random things I like. You can also organize your charms around a theme (animals, for example, or nature, food, silhouettes of family and friends, letters that spell out a word, even names. You can do shapes, you can do a "Tiffany"-style bracelet and load it with just one chunky heart, or you can do dog tags and have them engraved at a local jewelry store. This project encourages you to make up your own story and read it to the world through your piece. It also works on your sawing skills in the process.

My bracelet is in a sterling and copper mix. The charms are made from thicker metal, and special attention should be paid to finishing the edges so they are smooth. We don't want them cutting your wrist while the bracelet jingles around satisfyingly. Finally, I left the surface of the charms rough and matted the entire chain a bit with a Scotch-Brite pad. I wanted it to look well worn and well loved.

For this project, I designed a handmade toggle clasp (a bar that slides into a circle). However, if you've had it with sawing, you can simply buy an elegant premade toggle or lobster clasp and call it a day.

Make the Charms

1 Make templates first (page 153): Sketch a few designs that you'd like to make, then make perfect templates on graph paper. I recommend they be about ½"–1" (13mm–2.5cm) tall. Tinier shapes will be lost against the chain. Aim for about 6 charms, but of course, it's up to you. Cut out the templates carefully, apply the glue stick, and glue them to your sheet metal close together to minimize waste. Saw out each and shape with a file. Remove the paper templates.

2 Make a small divot at the top of each charm with the center punch. Insert a drill bit in the Dremel and drill the holes.

Make the Clasp

3 Measure about ¾" (2cm) from the corner along the edge of one side of your sheet, mark it, and measure ⅛" (3mm) from the edge. This will become the toggle bar for your clasp. Saw it out and smooth and straighten the edges with a file. Use a center punch to mark the bar at dead center between both sides and both edges. Drill a hole there.

4 Cut the 20g wire to 1⅛" (2.75cm). Form the wire into an oval, and hammer it flat. To build up tension in the metal so that the ends of the oval will spring together and stay put, gently open the ends of the link about ⅛"

(3mm). Now move the ends together, crossing one end over the other, and then cross them on the other side, making a side-by-side motion with your hands. Try closing the link. It should spring into shape. If not, repeat this step. You can also open the link from front to back a few times, again crossing one end on top of the other. The ends should now line up perfectly. Hammer them down to harden them so that the ends stay closed.

5 Insert a rubber wheel in the Dremel and smooth the edges of both the charms and the clasp until perfectly smooth. Use the tripoli buff and tripoli to polish, and then wash well with soap and water and dry. Repeat with the rouge buff and rouge. Wash well and gently pat dry with a paper towel.

Assemble the Bracelet

6 Lay out all the elements in front of you in the order you like. Insert each jump ring in the appropriate charm, thread the jump ring through the chain, and close it with the chain nose pliers.

7 Slip the oval toggle from step 4 onto the end of the chain. Thread a jump ring through the final link on the other end, and attach the toggle to the jump ring.

abstract triangle earrings

One 3½" x 3½" (9cm x 9cm) sheet 24g sterling, brass, or copper

Paper, pencil, and scissors

Glue stick

File

Beeswax, soap, or candle

Saw frame and blades

Center punch and hammer

Drill bit

Dremel with blue rubber wheel, tripoli buff, and rouge buff

Tripoli

Rouge

Hammer (optional, if a hammered finish is desired)

2 small jump rings approximately ⅛" (3mm) diameter

Premade ear wires in sterling silver or gold-filled, depending on metal used

Scotch-Brite pad (optional, to create matte finish)

Kinetics are fun. Not the kind you explored in high school physics; I mean in jewelry. When I describe a piece as "kinetic," I simply mean it has movement and life. These earrings provide a good introduction to both piercing metal *and* creating movement. Piercing metal is as simple as making cutouts within a form. We're starting big here—later projects in this chapter will call for tiny, possibly frustrating work—but for now, bigger is better. You can alter the scale of the earrings to suit your taste, or make them in mixed metals if desired. Although I made these in sterling, both brass and copper work equally well. Wear them with a low-cut blouse—they look best against a bare neck, though I also like them with hair away from the face. If your hair is long, wear it pulled back to let the earrings work their magic.

You can mix up the metals in this project with great results. I am partial to making these earrings with a sterling outer frame and brass inner element, or brass outer frame with copper interior.

Saw Out the Shapes

1 Start designing the earrings by making sketches of some abstract triangular shapes about 1¼" (3cm) wide by 2" (5cm) tall. You can use mine, of course (page 152), but it's always fun to extrapolate. Begin by drawing the outer element. Then design a middle element that will hang nicely within it. When you are happy, cut it out of the paper. Now do the same with the inner element, and cut it out.

2 Cut your metal in half, and glue the 2 halves together as you may have done with the Oval Earrings previously in this chapter (page 54). Let dry for 5 minutes. Now glue the template for the larger shape on the sheet. Let dry for 5 minutes.

3 Lubricate your saw blade with beeswax, soap, or a candle, and saw the outer edge of your outer element. Do not remove the paper model. {a}

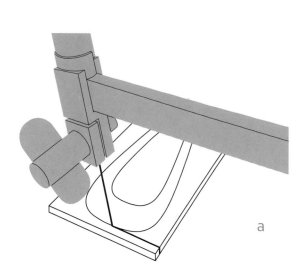

a

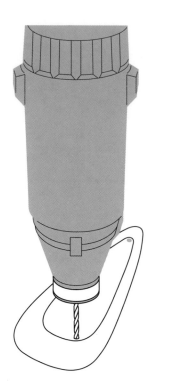

b

As outlined in the chapter opener (top of page 48), use your hammer and center punch or scribe to make a divot in your triangle just slightly away from the inner edge, about ⅛" (3 mm). Insert a drill bit in your Dremel and drill a hole where you've made the divot. {b} Open up the top thumbscrew of your saw frame to release the blade on one end. Insert the blade up through the hole in your metal, and reattach the blade to the saw frame. This is tricky: The piece will be like a bead on a string, but be careful to not let it dangle from the saw blade, as it will likely break the blade. {c}

Lubricate your saw blade with beeswax, soap, or a candle. Saw out your inner portion of the triangle, open the thumbscrew of your saw frame to release the blade, and then pull it out. When you are done, remove the paper model and clean up both the inner edges and the outer edges with a file. The best way to tackle the inner edges is to rest the piece flat on your bench with a bit hanging over the side and use an up-and-down motion with the half-round side of the file. This sort of shaping is the only time you may have to file in both directions.

Glue your second template onto the piece of metal left over from sawing the outer element, and saw it out. File as in step 5. Check to make sure the inner element has enough room around it so it won't bump the outer element when assembled. We want freedom of movement here! File the edges smooth, and pry apart the sheets.

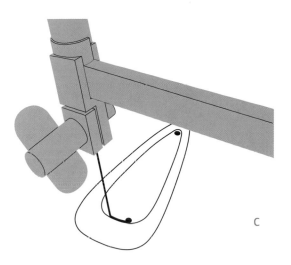

c

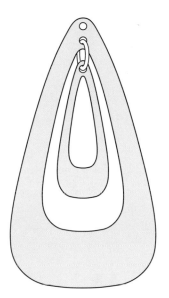

d

7 If desired, hammer the outer element so it juxtaposes with the inner element. (For practice with hammering, try making the Hammered Disc Earrings on page 51, or see step 5 of that project for specific hammering instructions.) Make sure you are working on the correct side of each earring so the two will make a pair of mirror shapes, rather than two of the same shape. For a matte finish, use a Scotch-Brite pad to methodically scrub both sides of each piece of metal *in one direction* only.

Drill the Holes

8 With a permanent marker, indicate at the top of the triangle where you will drill the holes for the ear wires. Then mark a second hole directly beneath the one from which the jump ring will hang (from which, in turn, the inner element will hang). Drill both holes on each earring.

9 Smooth both the inner edges and the outer edges of your elements with the rubber wheel in your Dremel. Now smooth the inner circle with the rubber wheel. Insert your tripoli buff and then polish the surface with tripoli. Wash and dry everything well and repeat with a rouge buff and rouge. Wash well and gently pat dry with a paper towel.

Assemble the Earrings

10 Open a jump ring and insert it through the bottom hole of one of the earrings. Thread the inner piece on it and close the jump ring. Repeat with the second earring. {d}

chandelier earrings

Earrings dripping with beads are all the rage, but a little-known fact is that they have been a staple of jewelry making across all cultures for centuries. Etruscan jewelry is replete with dangly forms. Renaissance earrings often incorporate elaborate pearl drops. The Victorians loved the complicated in all manner of style, from clothing to furnishings, and the intricate jewelry of that period took inspiration from the baroque styles of the 17th century, as well as from ethnic styles newly discovered during the apex of imperial expansion. North African jewelry in general embraces embellishment with drops, beads, and enameled shapes. Northern Indian jewelry tinkles with silver bells, and antique Turkoman jewelry practically rings with the sound of symbolic elements and bells hanging from every piece.

But enough of the history lesson. Chandelier earrings are jangly and fun and can be made in all styles, from delicate to chunky, dainty to bold. This project takes a cue from a baroque style of earring comprising two ornate shapes that then invite adornment with tons of beads. The earrings pictured mix up the styles, shapes, and colors of the beads, but do what you like to get the effect you want. These are in sterling, but brass looks rich, golden, and gorgeous, too.

ADVANCED INTERMEDIATE

3" x 3½" (7.5cm x 8.5cm) 20g sterling or brass sheet

2' (61cm) 28g brass or sterling wire

Tracing paper, pen, and scissors

Glue stick

Beeswax, soap, or candle

Saw frame and blades

File

Sheets of sandpaper in 220 through 600 grit

Center punch and hammer

Drill bit

Dremel with blue rubber wheel, tripoli buff, and rouge buff

Tripoli

Rouge

Round nose pliers

Chain nose pliers

8 beads of your choosing

8 jump rings about ⅛" (3mm) diameter

Premade ear wires in sterling silver or gold-filled, depending on metal used

Saw Out the Shapes

1 Using the templates (page 153) as a guide, trace onto graph paper using a pen. These templates are considerably more intricate than what we've done so far, so draw a square around the design and cut *that* square out first. Glue the square piece onto your metal. Lubricate your saw blade with beeswax, soap, or a candle. Saw out the 2 shapes. You may be tempted to double up your metal and cut both pieces at once; however, unlike previous projects, this shape is very complex, so it may be easier to

do them separately. Plus, I *want* you to do it twice for practice! File and shape to perfection. If necessary, cut a small triangular piece of 220-grit sandpaper, roll it into a small cone, and use it like dental floss to clean up the small curves of the earrings. Follow this by making triangles in 300–600 grit, and use them to smooth the shape perfectly. Then use the smoothed shapes as templates for the second pair. Glue them on. Lubricate your saw blade with beeswax, soap, or a candle, and saw those out. Shape as before.

Drill the Holes

2 Use your center punch and hammer to mark holes for the ear wires, beads, and the 2 points where the top element attaches to the bottom one. Each top element will have 4 holes—1 in the dead center at the top for the ear wire and 3 below it (1 in the middle for the bead and 2 where the elements are attached). Each bottom element will have 2 holes at the top points and 3 at the bottom points, for the beads. Be methodical in this step and really try to make all the holes evenly apart and the same distance from the edge of the metal. {a} Insert a drill bit in the Dremel and drill the holes as described in the chapter opener (page 48).

3 Polish the earrings with the rubber wheel. Insert your tripoli buff in the Dremel and polish with tripoli. Wash and dry well. Insert your rouge buff and polish with rouge. Wash well and gently pat dry with a paper towel.

Assemble the Earrings

4 Choose your beads and arrange them on your bench as they will be hung on the earrings. Fasten each bead to the earring components as described in step 3 of the Long Twig Earrings with Beads (page 27).

NOTE We fasten the beads before assembling the earring because it's far easier to do this before the pieces are assembled.

5 Open your jump rings, insert them in the points of the 2 top elements, and join the top elements to the bottom ones. Add your ear wires.

industrial earrings

industrial earrings

I took my cue for these earrings from a stainless steel sheet drilled with holes used by an architect to make a contemporary stair railing. This kind of pattern is found all over the industrial world, from grating used over heaters to perfectly machined gears and plates. Rather than trying to replicate the holes in a perfectly machined style, I opted for a free-form look. While randomness in life can be problematic, in these earrings, it's preferred. We're talking about drilling many holes in a random pattern, and then using a saw to enlarge some of them to hang beads within. This project is relatively simple but time consuming because you're being introduced to piercing out tiny circles within the earrings, so it's a perfect exercise in patience! I opted for rather large circles at 1½" (3.8cm) in diameter, but choose the size you like. Giant is great too, for lots of drama. These earrings work in brass or sterling.

INTERMEDIATE

1⅝" x 3¾" (4cm x 9.5cm) 24g sheet of sterling or brass

1' (30.5cm) 24g, 26g, or 28g sterling or brass wire

Round templates

Graph paper, pencil, and scissors

Glue stick

Center punch and hammer

Beeswax, soap, or candle

Saw frame and blades

File

Drill bits in 3 different sizes

Sheets of sandpaper in 220–600 grit

Dremel with blue rubber wheel, tripoli buff, and rouge buff

Tripoli

Rouge

Tiny beads of your choosing (I recommend those with a diameter of no more than ⅛" [3mm])

Round nose pliers

Chain nose pliers

Premade ear wires in sterling silver or gold-filled, depending on metal used

Saw Out the Shape

1 Using a template (page 152), draw two 1½" (3.8cm) circles on graph paper. Carefully cut out and glue to your sheet. Saw both pieces out and leave the templates on the sheet. Gently file the edges until perfectly round, using the template as a reference. Remove the paper.

Drill the Holes

2 Use your center punch and hammer to make a multitude of divots throughout the piece. More is better here, as is truly random spacing. Insert the drill bit in your Dremel and drill the hole with the middle size of your 3 drill bits. {a}

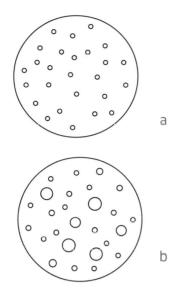

a

b

3 You want the holes to be of differing sizes, otherwise it gets boring. Choose those you want to be bigger, and enlarge them with the larger of your 2 remaining drill bits. {b}

4 You'll want to further enlarge some holes so that you can dangle beads within them. On those holes, use your templates or a permanent marker to draw differently sized circles around the holes you choose—I like ¼" to ⅜" (6mm–9.5mm) size. Be sure to enlarge the hole far enough away from any holes above them so there will be enough space to drill a hole for a bead. Open up the top thumbscrew of your saw frame to release the blade on one end. Insert the blade up through the hole in your metal, and reattach the blade to the saw frame. Lubricate the blade with beeswax, soap, or a candle. Saw out the circle. Be prepared to work in small areas. You will be turning your piece around a lot. You may break more blades than you wish to count because of the necessity of maneuvering within a tiny space, but don't worry.

5 When the holes are complete, file them smooth by one of two methods: 1) If they are large enough to insert the tip of your file, use the half-round side to make them even; or 2) cut a small triangular piece of 220-grit sandpaper, roll it into a small cone, and use it like dental floss to clean up the small curves of the earrings. Follow this by making triangles of 300–600 grit, and use them to smooth the holes perfectly.

6 Use the smallest of your drill bits to make holes above the enlarged spaces in which you will dangle beads.

7 Smooth the outer edges of the pendant with a rubber wheel and Dremel, and then use your tripoli buff and tripoli. Wash well and dry. Use your rouge buff and rouge to shine. Wash and dry the earrings and gently pat dry with a paper towel.

8 Add beads as described in step 3 of the Long Twig Earrings with Beads in chapter 1 (page 27). Slip on the ear wires.

arts and crafts pendant with bead

ADVANCED INTERMEDIATE

2⅝" x 1¼" (6.5cm x 3cm) sheet 22g sterling silver or copper

Tracing paper, pencil, pen, and scissors

Glue stick

Beeswax, soap, or candle

Saw frame and blades

File

Center punch and hammer

Drill bit

Dremel with blue rubber wheel, tripoli buff, and rouge buff

Tripoli

Rouge

3" (7.5cm) 24g, 26g, or 28g wire sterling silver or copper wire

Wire cutters

Round nose pliers

Chain nose pliers

Scotch-Brite pad (optional, use to create a matte finish)

Jump ring in sterling silver or copper

Premade chain in a matching metal

Bead of your choosing

Arts and Crafts is one of my favorite styles in art. Replete with organic forms, swirling lines, and cutouts, the jewelry especially is sensuous and evocative of nature. Although it originated in the 1890s, its influence is still felt everywhere in jewelry. I've modified a classic "Jugendstil" motif of an abstract scarab shape for our pendant here. While there are only a few steps to this pendant, it differs from earlier projects in this book because you have to pierce out very precise and defined shapes within small areas. I prefer to make this pendant in either silver or copper, as these metals, although considered humble at the time, were staples of Arts and Crafts jewelry. The bead at the bottom is your choice, although I recommend either a classic Arts and Crafts oval shape in a shade of blue or a freshwater pearl. Because the lines of this pendant are so classic and welcoming, it makes a wonderful gift for any jewelry-loving friend. It looks lovely with flowing dresses that evoke the delicacy of the form.

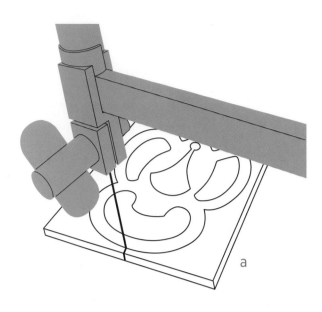

a

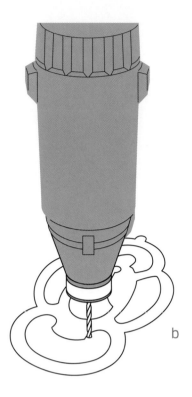

b

Saw Out the Shape

1 Trace the template on page 152 onto tracing paper. If you're feeling artistic, make a sketch of your own! Draw a square around the design and cut that out. With the glue stick, glue the piece to your metal sheet. Let dry for 5 minutes. Lubricate your saw blade with beeswax, soap, or a candle, and saw the outer shape. {a}

2 Use your center punch and hammer to create a divot near the inner edge of one of the large spaces of the pendant where the cutouts will be. Keep the hole near the lines so that you don't waste extra time sawing from the hole to the line that you wish to cut. Insert your drill bit in the Dremel and drill the holes. Repeat with the other 4 inner areas. {b}

3 Lubricate the saw blade with beeswax, soap, or a candle. Open up the top thumbscrew of your saw frame to release the blade. Insert the blade up through the hole in your metal, and reattach the blade to the saw frame. The piece will be like a bead on a string. Be careful to not let it dangle from the saw blade, as it's likely to break it. Working very slowly and carefully, saw the shapes within the pendant. You will be turning your piece around a lot in very tight areas. Always keep your saw moving in a gentle up-and-down motion, no matter how tight the turn. In some cases, you will be turning your piece 180 degrees! {c}

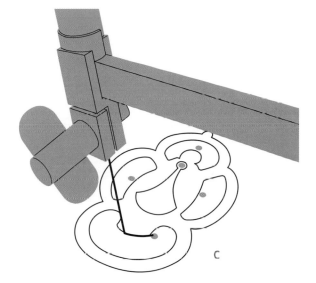

c

d

Assemble the Necklace

4 Now cut a Scotch-Brite pad into a thin strip about 1/16" wide x 3" long (2mm x 7.5cm), and smooth the edges with it. Yes, it's ridiculously thin, but it's necessary so that you can wiggle it into your cutouts and use it just like dental floss to clean up the edges. You can also use a sandpaper cone in a similar manner as described in step 1 of the Chandelier Earrings (page 75) and a file in the larger areas.

5 Smooth the outside edge of your pendant with a rubber wheel inserted in the Dremel, and polish the whole thing with tripoli and rouge as described above.

6 At the top, use your permanent marker to indicate where to drill the hole for your bail (the jump ring through which your chain will hang). Use your center punch and hammer to make a divot, insert the drill bit in the Dremel, and drill the hole. Insert and close a jump ring.

7 Cut a piece of wire about 3" (7.5cm) long for the bead. Using your round nose pliers, loop one end into a tiny curl on which the bead will rest when strung, and add your bead as in step 3 of the Long Twig Earrings with Beads in chapter 1 (page 28). {d}

8 Slip the pendant onto a premade chain and enjoy!

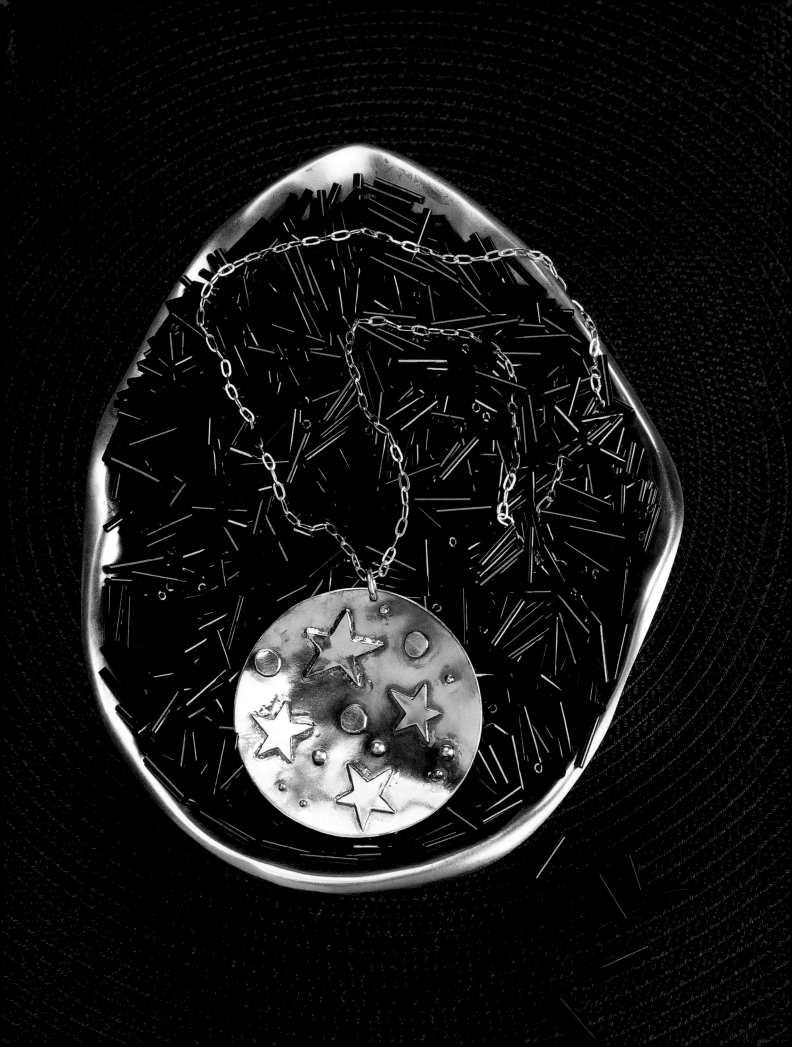

three

the mini torch

You are ready to make the leap. So far you have been making sophisticated jewelry using "cold connections"—joining pieces without solder. But you long for more. You're ready to make a commitment. You've met the right one, and it's beckoning you. You want the heat, the fun, and the excitement of . . . the butane mini torch.

If you think that using a drill is thrilling, wait until you start soldering! There is a timeless fascination with heating up metal and watching it glow, melt, or otherwise change. Even though I've done it thousands of times, I am still psyched every time I make a perfect solder joint or melt metal into interesting shapes. And you should see my students on the first day of class when they learn to use a torch—it's so great to witness, over and over again, the awe, wonderment, and power they feel.

In this chapter, you will learn the basics of soldering. I outline it just as I teach it in my classes. My directions will make it easy, nonthreatening, and, most of all, fun.

After I go over the basics of using the torch, I have some simple exercises for you to do to practice and get comfortable.

Mini Torch

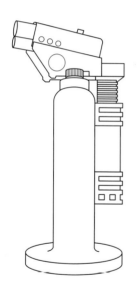

The best way to think about a mini torch is as a giant lighter. Thinking of it in this way both demystifies it and makes the way it works easier to grasp. People hear "solder" and they freak, overwhelmed by images of sparks flying, things burning, I-beams, copper pipe. Banish these images from your mind and approach soldering as if it were merely a matter of lighting a candle.

The first thing you need to do to begin soldering is to fill your torch with butane. First, turn the torch so that it's upside down. Next, place the nozzle of the butane can onto the fill valve in the middle of the torch base. *Do not push yet!* Now, while firmly holding both the torch and the can, press them together and count to four—not too fast, not too slow. The goal is to fill, but not to overfill, the torch with fuel. Overfilling can lead to problems in using the torch due to the excess gas—dangerous!

Now, practice turning on your torch. There are two common designs of butane torches. One has an ignition plunger and a knob that controls the gas flow; the other, a trigger-style starter and a locking slider for hands-off operation. Follow the directions for your particular model and practice until you can do it smoothly. The biggest difference between models is how you actually control the amount of air and the flow of gas. Trigger models use a lever on top of the torch head to control airflow. To get a hot, pointy flame, which is what you want, the lever must be all the way to the left. No bushy flames like a traditional lighter—after all, we're not at an arena concert.

For knob and plunger models, there is a small black plastic collar with two holes in it on top of the torch head. These holes must be aligned with the corresponding holes in the torch head in order to light the torch and to attain a hot, pointy flame. You can rotate the black collar to see the alignment holes underneath. The knob that you open to ignite the torch (on the left side of the torch head) controls the gas flow just like the side lever on the trigger model. The black collar controls airflow just like the top lever on the trigger model.

I *have* to stress safety in this chapter. Sure, you can drill your finger or file into your palm—but those injuries, while painful, are not particularly life threatening. Setting something on fire through negligence is. Never get cavalier when using a mini torch; do not think, "I'm just going to leave it on while I get this other piece ready." Though small, a mini torch burns at around 2,500 degrees Fahrenheit (1,204°C). That's pretty hot. It's hotter than any oven I've ever used, and you know what kind of damage an oven can inflict not only to your cake but also to your hands and face. Please *be careful* and handle the torch with due respect.

If you haven't already, set up your bench with a charcoal block in the middle on a heatproof surface. A thick ceramic plate or inverted baking pan works fine. Another tip I learned from a student is to use a small piece of fireproof blanket, which can be had from any jewelry supply store. Clear your bench of any paper products or extraneous matter. Make sure you have a ceramic or metal bowl of water close at hand.

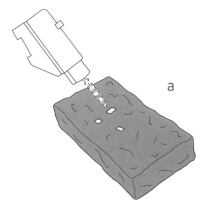

a

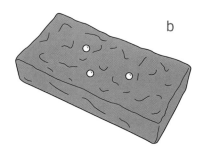

b

Let's begin. Cut yourself a ¼" x ¼" (6mm x 6mm) piece of 24g sterling sheet; place it on your charcoal; turn on your torch; and, using a smooth back-and-forth motion over the silver only, heat it up. The metal will turn dark, then begin to buckle at the corners, and finally roll itself up into a little gray ball. Pick it up with tweezers and cool it in the water (I'll call this "quenching" from now on). Examine with pride. Cut a couple more pieces and practice: Just heat the piece, and then cool it. Then continue to heat it and watch what happens. Then heat it even more until the metal crawls together and forms a ball. Make another ball, and some more. . . . {a} and {b} You have done three steps in this simple exercise: 1) You have annealed your metal, meaning you have heated it up until it's softened; 2) you have begun to melt it; and 3) you have made "shot," those cute little balls you're going to love using.

TIP When you first start to make balls, you will find that they have a tendency to want to escape from the flame and roll off your charcoal block. Make it difficult for them to do this: Use a scribe to dig a thick line about ¼" (6mm) away from the edge, all the way around the block. This creates a nice ditch that will catch the errant balls and save you a lot of heartache (as well as charred spots on your bench).

Finally, sometimes the balls just will never look right. Simply reheat the unattractive ones until they re-ball and see whether they are better. One trick I learned through trial and error is this: when your ball is done, pull your torch *straight up* from the ball very slowly. For some reason this helps keep the ball round.

Put them aside until you are ready to clean them with pickle—but safety first:

Safety Tips

1 Always light the torch away from your face, and away from any objects. I like to hold it in the air and aim it away from me at about shoulder height. Sometimes I see students lighting the torch downward on their bench—bad idea! It goes without saying that this is a fire hazard.

2 Be careful to not handle the torch by its tip. Even though it does not stay oven-hot after you use it, it can still be hot enough to startle you and make you drop it.

3 Always keep your bench clear of all paper products when you are soldering. This is not negotiable. Put your bills and fashion magazines elsewhere for now.

4 When you quench your piece, be sure to leave it in the water for a few seconds. Balls in particular have a nasty habit of not cooling off all the way through if you simply dunk and remove them. I can't tell you how many times I burned a finger when just starting out by quickly quenching a ball in water and immediately scooping it up with my fingers, only to realize that I'm holding a piece of metal that is still blazing hot on the inside—ouch!

5 Finally, while this sounds obvious, it's easy to forget: When you are soldering—and really, in doing anything using a tool—always focus your *entire* attention on what you are doing. Letting your mind wander is a sure-fire way to melt your piece and otherwise create a potentially dangerous situation.

Pickle

The balls are round-ish and cute. But they're also gray (the gray is oxidation, or fire-scale, caused by oxygen bonding to the metal when it is heated). Who wants that? We crave shiny silver! This is where your pickle comes in. Pickle, a weak acid solution, cleans the silver—or copper or brass—after it has been heated. It removes discoloration and readies the piece for polishing or for the next soldering step.

To make pickle, fill your Crock-Pot with water, and add about 1 teaspoon (5mL) of Sparex #2 or another pickle solution. Plug it in and let it heat up. When it's warm, stir the pickle solution with a chopstick (or even with your copper tongs) until the Sparex dissolves.

NOTE Do not use any steel or other metal implements in your pickle. Only use your copper tongs or a stainless steel tea ball. If another metal is introduced to the solution, it "copperizes" the solution, and will leave a layer of copper over any piece that goes in. Ironically, the copper tongs don't do this. Having a piece copperized in the pickle is a bummer, because although it can be removed, to do so you either have to heat up the piece again or polish it like crazy. Better to avoid it.

Now see how the pickle works: Place the small balls you have just made in the tea ball, and place it carefully in the pickle—you don't want it to splash. Leave it there for a few minutes. My students always ask, "Victoria, how long do I leave my piece in the pickle?" I always respond, "Until it's clean." Nobody likes this answer. They want a precise time frame. But each batch of pickle is different, and each piece can react in a different way. To appease everyone, let's just say three minutes and leave it at that.

After you take your piece out of the pickle with the copper tongs, wash it thoroughly with an old toothbrush, soap, and water. Wash your hands while you're at it. After you dry your piece, it's ready to go on to the next step on its journey to becoming a piece of jewelry.

Safety Tips

1 Handle the pickle with care. Avoid splashing the solution on clothing, walls, and—most of all—your skin. While I have never seen someone actually injured by pickle, it is better to be safe than to be sorry.

2 A lesser-known fact is that pickle works even when cold. The scientific explanation is that since it's an acid, it works regardless of temperature. It just takes longer to clean the metal. If you are anxious about accidentally leaving your Crock-Pot on when you're done working, just leave it off. Add a little more Sparex #2 to the water and plan to have a bit of a longer wait between soldering steps.

3 Be sure to turn the pickle off when you're done for the day. The most dangerous aspect of pickling is leaving the Crock-Pot on overnight (or for days if you're really spaced out) so that all the water evaporates. Not only does this ruin the pot, but it also creates a fire hazard. When the water becomes low, simply refill and add another teaspoon (5mL) of Sparex #2. There is no need to empty out the solution each time unless it's really dirty.

SCRATCHING THE SURFACE

Ward off confusion about what sheet of solder is what by scratching a bunch of small H, M, or S's (E's) into the appropriate sheet with a scribe. Scratch a lot of letters so that even when you've used quite a bit of the sheet, you'll still know what it is. Better to know now than have your *piece* tell you when it comes apart during a step because you have not kept track of which solder has been used.

Solder

Once you have mastered the art of making balls, you're ready to think about solder. Solder is essentially a metal alloy used to fuse metallic surfaces. I work almost exclusively with sheet solder, and the directions in this book reflect that. If you do have wire solder, though, simply hammer the wire flat and snip off pieces accordingly so that it works like sheet solder.

Solder comes in sheets of hard, medium, and easy, each marked with an "H" "M," or "S" (for hard, medium, or soft, which we call Easy) at the top of the sheet. The names refer to the melting temperatures, not to how sturdy a solder joint they produce. By using different temperature solders for different portions of your soldering project, you minimize the chance of opening your previously soldered seams. Always begin your projects by using hard sheets. Then graduate to medium. You can use medium for a number of solders because for some reason the "new" piece of medium solder you apply melts at a lower temperature than the "old" medium already soldered on. In plainer language, joints soldered with medium solder don't tend to open up, even after repeated heating. Save easy solder for the very last step. Think of the different solders in the following way: When you begin something new, it's "hard"; a little ways down the road, it's "medium"; and when you've done it a lot, it's "easy."

Now that you know the differences, here's how to handle that solder. The pieces of solder you will use are small—tiny even, with many no more than ⅟₁₆" (1.5mm) square, and some are even smaller. The solder doesn't become square on its own. Here's how to cut it into little pieces, or "paillons," as we jewelers call them:

Using your shears, make a few ¼" (6mm) long cuts vertically from the bottom of your sheet about ⅟₃₂" (.75mm) apart. It should look like fringe. Now turn the sheet sideways and crosscut the fringe so that tiny little squares fall away. That's it. If possible, hold your index finger over the fringe so the solder pieces don't fly everywhere, never to be seen again. Depending on the kind of soldering you're doing, you will need to adjust the size of the pieces. If they need to be wider, just make your fringe fatter. If you need longer pieces, just snip deeper into the big sheet of solder. {c}

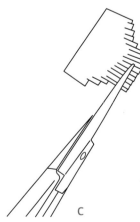

C

Flux

For jewelers, flux does not refer to an uncertain state of being. It's simply a chemical solution you apply with a paintbrush that keeps the solder and edges of metal clean so they will join well. I always recommend drying the flux with your flame before placing the solder on your piece—if you put chips of solder on wet flux, it will send them flying as it bubbles up while being heated. Then you have to start over—yawn.

As with any of the minor chemical solutions you use in silver jewelry making, handle your flux with care. Keep it capped when not in use, be careful to wipe it off your bench, and, of course, wash your hands thoroughly if they happen to come in contact with it.

A final thought about soldering: When you start soldering, you will overheat your piece from time to time, you will melt it, and, in fact, you will mess it up hopelessly and want to cry. Shed a tear, walk away from your bench, adjust your attitude to the "who cares" setting, and come back. Remember, that's why you're starting with brass, copper, and silver instead of gold! Breaking, ruining, wrecking, and destroying are all parts of the learning process in *any* craft. Try to accept it as part of the journey—a little bend in the road, if you will. Take it as you do any curve when driving: Ease gently into it, and then accelerate out.

A TIP I LEARNED DURING A MANICURE

Usually I zone out during a manicure or pedicure, but one day when I was feeling inexplicably alert, I checked out what the aesthetician was using to hold the nail polish remover. It was a little jar with a metal lid and springy plate that she tapped to release a small amount of polish remover. Wow, I thought, what a great container to use for flux! Well, turns out that the jewelry industry is miles ahead of me, because these little jars are widely used and available in jewelry supply stores. In addition to dispensing just the right amount of flux, they keep it clean and keep it from evaporating, thus minimizing waste.

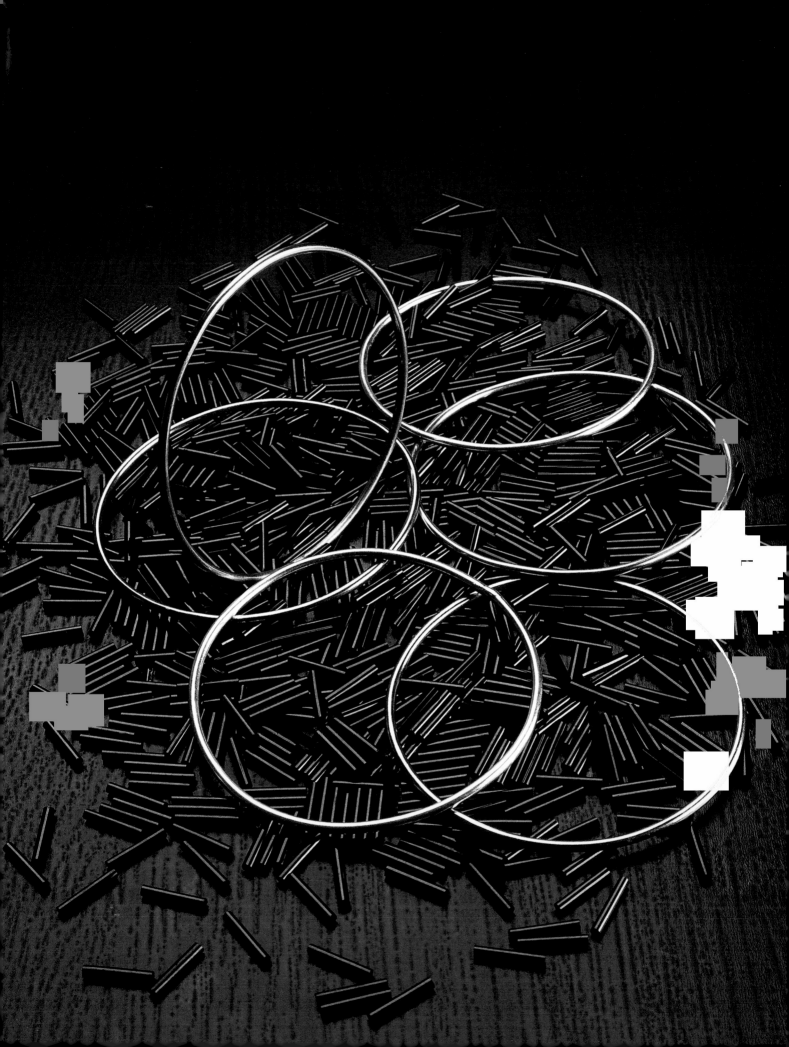

bangle set

A set of shiny bangles is a must in any jewelry wardrobe, and this set couldn't be easier. Made in sterling, copper, and brass, it fits with all styles and looks especially good in the summer, when your arm is likely to be bare and glistening in the sun.

From a technical standpoint, bangles primarily use the process of annealing, which you have just practiced in making the balls. Annealing is a technique whereby you add space between the molecules in the metal by heating them up so that the metal becomes flexible and easy to work with. Once annealed, metal will stay in that state until some sort of force is exerted upon it—like hammering or bending—at which point it starts to stiffen back up. Sometimes you need to anneal multiple times, as you may have to in this project. While annealing itself is not difficult, doing it repeatedly will build your confidence in using the mini torch for the more intense soldering experiences to come. These bangles are finished with a simple solder joint. By the time you are finished making them, you will be comfortable with your torch and ready to move on to some more delicate work.

INTERMEDIATE

17" (43cm) 12g sterling wire

17" (43cm) 12g copper wire

17" (43cm) 12g brass wire (or just pick 1 wire to use, and cut a length of 51" [129.5cm])

Wire cutters

File

Frozen juice can (frozen solid), spray deodorant can, or shaving cream can

Hammer

Charcoal block and heat-resistant surface like a ceramic dinner plate or metal baking pan

Mini torch

Flux and paintbrush

Shears

Sheet of easy solder

AA tweezers

Pickle and copper tongs

File

Dremel with blue rubber wheel, tripoli buff, and rouge buff

Tripoli

Rouge

NOTE With the brass and copper bangles, there will be a little silver seam where the piece is soldered. I recommend working only with silver solder because it's easier to flow than brass solder. However, if this seam bothers you, buy brass solder through a jewelry supply company.

Cut the Wire

1 Determine the length of wire needed to make your bangles. Most commercial bangles are 2¾" (7cm) in diameter. To get the circumference that corresponds with this, simply multiply 2¾" x 3.14 (in metric, 7cm x 3.14). For my purposes, you end up with a length of about 8" (20.5cm) if you have a small wrist, and approximately 8¼"–8½" (21cm–21.5cm) if you have a large wrist.

2 Cut your 3 wires to this length (2 lengths in each wire) and file the ends straight. You will have 6 pieces.

Anneal and Shape the Wire

3 Get out your charcoal and heat-resistant surface. Place a piece of wire on your charcoal block. It may hang over the edges a bit depending on what size charcoal block you buy.

4 For wire, the proper annealing technique is this: Light up your torch and, beginning with one end, heat the metal until you start to see a light orange glow. It will begin to get dark. Then, move slowly along the wire away from that area and heat the length of the wire in the same way until the whole piece is dark. It should be uniformly dark gray (or, if you're using brass or copper, muddy gold or dark brown). When you start annealing, you'll notice that the darkness sort of jumps ahead of your torch and starts to creep ahead before you actually move your torch; this is normal. Step back and admire your work. *Do not quench the wire.* When you quench sterling (or brass or copper) after heating it, you actually stiffen the metal back up, which is exactly what we do not want to do. Let it air cool instead and set aside. Heat the remaining lengths of wire the same way. {a}

NOTE The brass may take on a layer of copper when it's heated. Do not be alarmed—it will polish out. Also, be aware that the brass may be a little springier and more difficult to work with, so just stick with it.

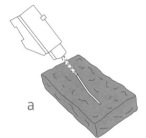

a

5 Using your copper tongs, transfer the wire pieces to the pickle. Wait for about 3 minutes. Then remove the wire from the pickle with your copper tongs, wash with soap and water, dry, and prepare to pound.

6 Place the juice can upright on your bench. Wrap 1 of your wires around the juice can, and press with your fingers until a semicircle shape is formed. Now place the juice can flat on the bench and hammer both ends toward the middle. Because it's been heated, the wire should be easy to shape. Get the ends to meet as closely as possible. Take the wire off the can.

TIP If the frozen juice can is really much too large for your bangle, consider using a frozen water bottle. Point is, find something cylindrical and hard to shape the bangles.

7 Using your hands, hold the wire by the ends and push the ends together over each other, first right over left, then left over right. This will build up tension in the metal so that the ends will spring together and stay there. You may need to anneal the metal once again. By the second time you've annealed, cooled, and pickled, you should be able to get the ends together perfectly. File them so they are flush. You don't want any gaps, because then the solder will not flow properly. {b} Take your time, but don't worry if the metal gets out of shape for now—we will fix this later. At this point, check the bangle for size. If it's a little too big—and it may be—saw off a little wire from one end, anneal, shape, and file again. Repeat this process with the other 5 pieces of wire. Check the wires to be sure they are clean and free of grease, dirt, or frozen juice concentrate.

Solder the Wire

8 Place your bangle flat on the charcoal block with the seam directly in front of you. You will now "dry the flux with your flame" (page 93). Dip your brush into the flux, and apply a dab to the seam. Just plunk it on—you can't really use too much, but using too little may cause you problems. Now use your torch to heat up the flux until it puffs up and then goes flat again. The reason for doing this *before* adding the solder is that the flux *does* bubble. If you have solder on your piece, the bubbling will blow it away, and you'll have to cut another piece.

9 Using your shears, cut a piece of solder into a small square that is about $\frac{1}{16}$" (1.5mm) square. With your AA tweezers (not your hand—remember, the bangle is hot!), place the solder on the charcoal directly underneath the seam. It should stick out just a little on both sides and must touch the wire. If there is too much, you'll have a lot of clean up to do after you solder; if there is too little, you'll have to fill in the gap with more solder {c}.

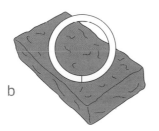

b

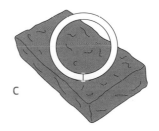

c

10 Light your torch. Hold it at a 45-degree angle and begin heating the entire bangle by moving it in a circle. This is called "preheating," and you should do it to every piece that requires soldering because it speeds up the process. Except for the area to which you have applied flux, the bangle will slowly darken. Preheat for about 30–45 seconds. Then, holding the torch at a 90-degree angle to your piece, move it side to side across the seam. You will see the solder jump up and fill in the seam with a shiny line. Make sure the solder flows all the way through the seam before pulling your torch away. Turn off your torch, and let the bangle air cool (again, do not quench). Pickle as before. Repeat with the other 5 bangles.

11 When the bangles are clean from pickling, remove them with your copper tongs, wash well with soap and water, and inspect the seams. They should be tightly joined, with no space between the seams. Hold them up to the light and make sure you can't see any light coming in through the seam. Now grab your juice can again and hammer the bangles around it to re-round them and to harden the metal so that the bangles stay in shape.

12 Smooth over the soldered seam with your Dremel's rubber wheel if necessary. Then polish the entire bangle with tripoli and rouge. Wash well with soap and water and gently pat dry.

You have mastered your first soldering project! On to bigger and better . . . or rather, smaller and more complicated.

circle and disc necklace

circle and disc necklace

INTERMEDIATE

12" (30.5cm) 16g sterling silver, brass, or copper wire

1¾" x 1¾" (4.5cm x 4.5cm) sheet 20g sterling, brass, or copper

3' (91cm) sterling silver chain of your choice

Pen with a diameter of about ½" (13mm) or a bit smaller

Round templates or graph paper, pencil, and scissors

Wax, soap, or candle

Saw frame and blades

Chain nose pliers

File

Charcoal block and heat-resistant surface like a ceramic dinner plate or metal baking pan

Mini torch

Flux and paintbrush

AA tweezers

Shears

Sheet of easy solder

Pickle and copper tongs

Center punch and hammer

Dremel with blue rubber wheel, tripoli buff, and rouge buff

Wire cutters

Ruler

Premade jump rings that match your chain

Premade lobster clasp that matches your chain (or make your own clasp as in step 7 of the Omega Chain [page 37])

Silver polishing cloth

This necklace is an almost literal take on one of my bestsellers of all time, the Circle Chain Disc Necklace I created in 2005. Long, lean necklaces are all the rage right now—and they show no signs of waning in popularity. Indeed, designed right, a long necklace can become a short necklace when the styles change . . . or when your mood (or wardrobe) dictates. This 40" (101.5cm) long necklace can be doubled-up into a shorter chain. Completed with a lobster clasp, its simplicity and understated elegance have been copied by many. You can mix up the metals if you like, and the style of chain is up to you. Curb chains work well, as they are somewhat flat. So are "regular" round chains. Just make sure the jump rings you create or buy go through the links.

This project is great for practicing your soldering skills. Using the techniques you learned in steps 9 and 10 of the Bangle Set on page 97, you will make smaller rings that are then hammered and linked to a premade chain. The small size of the rings ramps up the skill level. If you follow the steps below, by the time you are finished, you will have soldered no fewer than 26 times. There is sawing too, and cutting chain (a no-brainer). An abundant amount of jump-ring soldering adds to the mix. This necklace isn't harder than any other piece you've made so far. It may be a little labor-intensive, but it's bound to become one of your favorite go-to pieces.

Make the Rings

1 Make rings using your wire and pen as you learned if you made the Mixed-Metal Chain with Pendant in chapter 2 (page 58). See steps 1–4 of that project for specific instructions, but here is a recap: Wrap the end of the wire around the barrel and continue to do so until you have a nice coil of 7 links. Slide the coil off the pen. Holding it perpendicular to you and resting on your bench, carefully saw through the coil so that the rings separate. File the edges of each ring smooth, if necessary.

2 Using the same technique with which the Bangle Set on page 94 was soldered, solder the rings together (see steps 3–10 of the Bangle Set for a recap). Pickle, wash with soap and water, and dry.

3 Hammer the rings until you have a nice, faceted finish. (For practice with hammering, try making the Hammered Disc Earrings on page 51, or see step 6 of that project for specific hammering instructions.) Set aside for now; you'll polish later.

Make the Discs

4 Cut your sheet metal in half and glue the 2 halves on top of each other as you did with the Oval Disc Earrings with Dangles (page 54). Let dry. Use a round template to draw three ½" (13cm) circles on the sheet metal, or make a paper template as you learned if you made the Hammered Disc Earrings (page 51). Glue the templates on your sheet metal. Lubricate the saw blade with beeswax, soap, or a candle, and saw out the 3 discs. Refine the edges with a file, and then pry apart the sheets of metal.

5 Hammer the discs (again, see step 6 of the Hammered Disc Earrings on page 53).

Assemble the Necklace

6 Using a center punch with a hammer, mark divots where you will drill holes on opposite sides of the circles and discs. Be sure to line your holes up exactly opposite one another, or else the elements will hang crooked. Use your Dremel to drill the holes. Polish the pieces with a rubber wheel, followed by tripoli and rouge. Be sure to polish the back of each piece as well, as the style of the necklace makes both sides visible. Wash well and dry.

7 Lay your chain straight on your bench. Use a ruler to measure 2" (5cm) sections, and cut with wire cutters. Be sure to pick off any opened links at the ends. Cut 11 pieces of 2" (5cm) wire. Now, cut two pieces of 4" (10cm) wire.

8 Use your chain nose pliers to open one of the jump rings. Thread it through one of your circles and then through one of the 4" (10cm) pieces of chain. Close with the pliers. Repeat using a disc and a 2" (5cm) length of wire. Continue alternating circles and discs with 2" (5cm) pieces of chain, attaching the last one to a 4" (10cm) length of wire. Attach your clasp in the same manner. Buff the chain with a polishing cloth to remove any fingerprints.

cross earrings

Sticklers may say that these aren't cross-shaped earrings, but I did have that classic symbol in mind when I designed them. I must have been in a "Middle Ages" kind of mood, because this design has an openwork feel that certainly harks back to an earlier time. Maybe it's the stained glass look . . . at any rate, this soldering project has an old-world look that is accomplished with a whole bunch of solder joints. We are using a technique here called "butt soldering." I know, somewhat crude, but I swear it's the technical term! Basically, butt soldering is where you solder two pieces side by side. For these earrings, you have to gently file flat each area that is going to be soldered so that there is a good meeting point for the joint. If you don't do this, it's very difficult to have a strong solder joint, and the rings may snap off at each joint when you polish them—or worse, when you wear them.

I prefer these earrings in sterling; I think brass and copper come off as too "homemade" in this style. That said, I did leave them a little rough—too perfect, and they look machine made. Add on some beads for a little flair, and you have timeless style—think Lady Guinevere in jewels and gown, minus the constricting corset. Speaking of clothes, these earrings *do* look great with an evening dress!

INTERMEDIATE

18" (45.5cm) 16g sterling wire

15" (38cm) 18g sterling wire

Thick ballpoint or gel pen with about ¼" (6mm) diameter

Chopstick, pen, or thick nail with about ⅛" (3mm) diameter

File

Beeswax, soap, or candle

Saw frame and blades

Charcoal block and heat-resistant surface like a ceramic dinner plate or metal baking pan

Mini torch

Flux and paintbrush

AA tweezers

Scribe

Shears

Sheet of hard solder

Sheet of medium solder

Sheet of easy solder

Pickle and copper tongs

Tea ball

Dremel with blue rubber wheel, tripoli buff, and rouge buff

Tripoli

Rouge

Premade sterling silver ear wires

Make the Rings

1 Make 8 rings with the 16g wire and the larger of the 2 pens using the skills learned in the Mixed-Metal Chain with Pendant (page 58—see steps 1–4 of that project for specific instructions). Wrap the end of the 16g wire around the barrel of the pen and continue to do so until you have a nice coil of 8 loops. Slide the coil

a

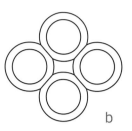

b

off the pen. Holding it perpendicular to you and resting it on your bench, lubricate your saw blade with beeswax, soap, or a candle and carefully saw through the coil so that the rings separate.

2 Repeat with the 18g wire and the smaller pen to make 8 smaller rings.

Solder

3 Solder your rings just as you did in steps 3–9 of the Bangle Set (page 96). Basically, we are performing the same technique, but the stakes are raised because the metal is much thinner and therefore has a higher chance of becoming overheated. Here is a recap: Place the ring on your charcoal block with the seam facing you. Apply a drop of flux to the joint, and dry with your torch. Cut a tiny, almost microscopic, piece of hard silver. Use your tweezers to place it beneath the seam on the charcoal block. Light your torch and carefully preheat the ring by holding the torch above it and moving it around the ring. Now concentrate the heat on the joint and wait for the solder to jump up and fill it. Quench the ring in water and set aside.

Repeat until you have 16 rings. Place the rings in the tea ball and pickle.

4 Pick a side of each ring to solder, and carefully file just at the point where the 2 circles will butt up against each other. *Get it?!* {a} Now place 4 of your larger rings in a clover pattern as in my example, with the flattened areas next to one another. Try to make sure the seams are *against the next ring*. It's easier to hide a seam when it's backed up against others than when it's standing out on the edge of the ring all on its own. Dab some flux with a paintbrush on the point where each ring meets the others on the curve (about ¼ of the way around the ring). Dry the flux with your flame (see page 97). {b}

5 Cut 4 tiny small pieces of medium solder. Use your tweezers to place a piece on top of each of the joints where 2 rings meet. It's helpful to angle the solder so that one edge is held angled within the seam itself.

6 Make sure you have a scribe at hand in case you need to poke a piece of solder or an errant ring back into place. Light up your torch and carefully heat the piece from the top, always making a circular motion with your hand.

TIME IS ON YOUR SIDE

Jump rings, necklace clasps, ear wires, and other elements are staples of the jewelry-making world. I firmly believe that all jewelers should learn to make these ubiquitous pieces by hand. However, I also believe in the constructive use of one's time. So as counter-intuitive as it seems, I recommend buying premade elements once you *have* learned to make these pieces by hand. Sometimes it's just not a good use of your time to spend half an hour making jump rings, for example. You should know *how* to make them, but you should also learn when it's okay to cut corners in the interest of time. Though it might save you a little money to make your own jump rings, the time it takes sometimes cancel out any of the gains.

Then concentrate the heat on one of the joints and hold it until the solder melts. Move the torch along to the next one until all 4 joints are soldered shut. Quench and pickle. Repeat with the other earring.

NOTE If your piece shifts while you're soldering and you end up soldering 2 places that you won't want, don't panic. The easy fix is to apply some flux to that area and heat the piece again. When the solder melts, simply pull the 2 pieces apart with a tweezers. Pickle and start afresh.

7 Now solder on the 4 small rings: This time, cut tiny pieces of easy solder, which flows at a lower temperature than medium and thus minimizes metal meltdown and the opening of previously soldered seams. Still, be careful when you heat your piece: 18g wire is quite thin. The trick is to keep your torch away from the little ring as much as possible, and to hit that area when the piece is fully heated and ready to solder. Solder the rings on as described above, quench, and pickle.

8 You now have 2 beautiful cross-style earrings. Polish any obvious bumps and seams with your Dremel's rubber wheel. Next, use tripoli and rouge. Wash and dry well. Add premade ear wires at the top and feel like a princess.

TIP Leave these as is in their beautiful simplicity, or dress them up by adding beads to the small wheels at the side and bottom as I have, following the directions in the Long Twig Earrings with Beads on page 27. Another nice variation is to add a draped effect by attaching short lengths of chain to the little rings. Finally, if you crave the hammered look, gently hammer the earrings so they have more texture.

id bracelet

One of the most important—and sometimes vexing—soldering techniques concerns jump rings. I knew I wanted to teach how to solder jump rings in this book, but how? I could have designed the expected chain mail project, or made you solder eight million jump rings to create a chain, but those are a bore. Spirits dampened, mind exhausted, I turned to my friend David Feldman for help. David is not a jeweler himself, though he has many years' experience in the industry. But sometimes the best ideas come from an outside source. Quickly sketching a bracelet that meshes (bad pun) a masculine ID-style plate with feminine laced loops, he hit upon a winner. Part biker, part Barbie, this bracelet is a great amalgam of styles and sensibilities. It's tough, but with a soft side, too.

I made this one in sterling silver and used two thick curb chains on the back, but any metal and any kind of chain work just as well. You can texture the plate or leave it plain and ready to engrave, whether with a skull and crossbones or with a rose.

INTERMEDIATE

2¼" x 1" (5.5cm x 2.5cm) sheet 20g sterling, brass, or copper

18" (45.5cm) 22g sterling, copper, or brass wire

6" (15cm) premade heavy chain in matching metal

Ruler and permanent marker

Chopstick, pen, or thick nail about ⅛" (3mm) diameter

File

Beeswax, soap, or candle

Saw frame and blades

Frozen juice can

Paper towel or thin washcloth

Center punch and hammer

Drill bit

Dremel with blue rubber wheel, tripoli buff, and rouge buff

File

Charcoal block and heat-resistant surface like a ceramic dinner plate or metal baking pan

Mini torch

Flux and paintbrush

AA tweezers

Locking tweezers with weighted base

Shears

Sheet of medium solder

Pickle and copper tongs

Tripoli

Rouge

Premade lobster clasp

Silver polishing cloth

Make the Plate

1 Using the edge of your sheet metal, measure a shape about 2" wide by ¾" tall (5cm x 2cm). Imagine this size against your wrist: You may want to make it a bit smaller. Mark the shape with a permanent marker or scribe.

2 Lubricate your saw blade with beeswax, soap, or a candle, and saw the shape out. Use the file to gently round the corners so they do not cut into your wrist.

3   With a permanent marker, mark 4 holes to drill at each end of the plate. Be sure they are evenly spaced. Using the center punch and hammer, make divots for your drill. With a drill bit inserted in your Dremel, drill all 8 holes. {a}

4   Place your frozen juice can vertically to you on your bench, and place the middle of the plate on the can. Using your bare hands, bend the metal down around the can so it has a nice arc. You may want to wrap the can in a paper towel or thin washcloth so your hands don't freeze. Put the can away. Using your Dremel's rubber wheel, smooth all edges and surfaces.

Make the Jump Rings

5   Using the chopstick or pen, make 22 jump rings using the 20g wire as described in steps 1–4 of the Mixed-Metal Chain with Pendant (page 60). Here is a recap: Wrap the end of the wire around the chopstick or pen and continue to do so until you have a nice coil of 13 links. Slide the coil off the pen. Lubricate the saw blade with beeswax, soap, or a candle. Holding the coil perpendicular to you and resting it on your bench, carefully saw through it so that the rings separate. File the edges of each ring smooth if necessary. Repeat until you have made 22 rings.

Attach the Jump Rings to the Plate

6   Thread 1 ring through the outer hole on one side of the plate. Close it. Now put the ring upright in your locking tweezers so the seam faces up while the plate is resting on your

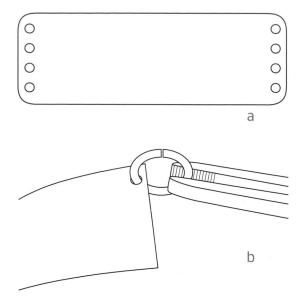

a

b

charcoal block. Try to position the tweezers so the ends are not close to the seam. If the ends are too close, they become a heat draw, and it will take you longer to solder the rings. The more heat you need to apply, especially to a thin little piece, the more likely you are to melt it. {b}

7   Dab some flux on the ring seam and dry with the torch. Cut some tiny pieces of medium solder and place them on the edge of your charcoal for safekeeping. Now use your paintbrush—the one that has a bit of flux still on it—to pick up a piece of solder. Place it on the seam carefully.

8   Light your torch and begin to heat up the ring slowly, keeping your flame well clear of the seam. Make sure that the remaining flux on the seam from applying the piece of solder dries without displacing the solder. Now move your flame closer and aim it at the side of the seam. The solder will begin to flow and spread across it. Quench the piece in water, immersing the entire plate, which has heated up during the soldering process. Dry it, and continue in the

same way to solder the remaining 3 links into the holes you drilled. {c}

9 Open another jump ring, thread it through the 2 upper rings hanging from the plate, and close it. Solder as above. {d} Thread another jump ring through the 2 lower rings, soldering the ring closed. Thread the next ring through the second ring that joins the 2 upper rings from the first row of rings, close, and solder. Then thread another ring through the second ring that joins the 2 lower rings from the first row. Now thread another ring through the ring that connects the 2 rings in the third row of rings, close, and solder. {e} Pickle the piece, wash, and dry.

10 Continue in this manner with the other side of the plate. Pickle as needed, wash, and dry.

Attach the Chain

11 Cut the chain into 2 pieces that will attach to the ringed plate to finish the bracelet. An average length would be about 2½" (6.5cm) each (or a bit more), but measure your wrist to be sure. Thread 1 of the remaining jump rings through the final jump ring attached to the plate, and then thread it through the chain. Close and solder. Repeat with the other side.

12 Use a jump ring to attach the clasp, and solder shut. Thread the remaining jump ring into the end of the second chain and solder it shut. Pickle the bracelet, wash with soap and water, and dry.

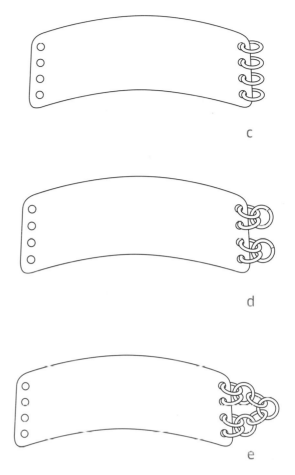

c

d

e

13 With your tripoli buff inserted in your Dremel, carefully polish the front of the plate and over the rings while holding the lace sides tight, being *very* careful to not let the rings and chain get caught in the spinning tool. Follow this with the rouge. Use a polishing cloth to shine up the chain, but *do not* attempt to polish the chain itself with the Dremel.

heart earrings

Matters of the heart can seem subtle and simple. But, as with anything, the devil is in the details. These heart earrings teach you how to solder a wire onto a sheet of metal, in this case, to make ear wires. It may sound easy, and—since you've mastered the jump ring if you have made the ID Bracelet (page 106)—the learning curve isn't *too* steep. But the kicker with this technique is that you'll be doing two very different things with your two hands at the same time. Moreover, you're going to have to do something with your nondominant hand that will feel awkward and strange. If you have played the piano or guitar, this may not be a big deal to you. Still, as with many of the projects in this chapter, the metal meltage factor can be high and, as a result, can breed frustration. However, stick with it, and, when you're done, you will have mastered one of the more delicate soldering techniques.

INTERMEDIATE

1¼" x 1¼" (3cm x 3cm) 20g sterling, brass, or copper sheet

3" (7.5cm) 20g sterling silver wire

Graph paper, pencil, and scissors

Glue stick

Beeswax, soap, or candle

Saw frame and blades

File

Wire cutters

Hammer

Charcoal block and heat-resistant surface like a ceramic dinner plate or metal baking pan

Mini torch

Flux and paintbrush

Shears

Sheet of easy solder

Locking tweezers (no weighted base)

AA tweezers

Copper tongs and pickle

Dremel with blue rubber wheel, tripoli buff, and rouge buff

Tripoli

Rouge

Silver polishing cloth (shiny finish)

Scotch-Brite pad (matte finish)

Saw Out the Hearts

1 Using graph paper and a pencil, draw a heart measuring about ¾" (2cm) tall (or use template on page 153). It's harder to work small, so this is good practice, too. Cut the heart out.

2 Lubricate your saw blade with beeswax, soap, or a candle, and saw your sheet of metal in half. Wash well with soap and water and dry thoroughly. Coat one half with a heavy coat of the glue stick, and glue the 2 halves

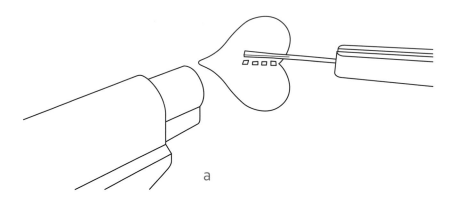

a

together. Place a large book or pot on top and let dry for 5 minutes. Coat your heart template with the glue stick and apply it to the sheet. Let dry for 5 minutes. Cut out with your saw. File the edges to shape. Pry apart the sheets.

3 Perform a preliminary polish: Insert the blue rubber wheel in your Dremel and polish the edges and the surfaces of the hearts, both front and back. Now follow with tripoli and wash and dry well. A final buff will be done later.

Make the Ear Wires

4 Cut your wire into two 1½" (3.8cm) pieces. Using the hammer, flatten about ¼" (6mm) of one end of each wire. This end will be soldered to the heart, and it's important to make the surfaces of the meeting point of the 2 pieces you're soldering together as flat as possible. This will make the soldering easier and the joint stronger. Now, file the end you have just hammered to a nice round shape—you do not want jagged edges. In addition to looking unattractive, the little frays are thinner than the rest of the piece, and therefore they will melt more quickly and

curl up, eventually melting more wire. Repeat with the other wire.

Solder

5 Get out your charcoal block and heat-resistant surface. Set the heart on your charcoal sideways and upside down so the back faces up. Place the heart so the V at the top is on the same side as your dominant hand. Dab some flux beneath the V and dry it with your torch. Now cut a few slivers of easy solder and place them on the edge of your charcoal.

6 Put the end of your wire in your locking tweezers with the flattened side out. Place it on your bench near your dominant hand. Use your tweezers to pick up a few pieces of solder and place them in a vertical line, starting at the V top of the heart. {a} Now light up your torch again and place it in your *nondominant* hand perpendicular to the upper portion of the heart. Yes, righties, this means the left hand. Lefties . . . you got it. Why switch up hands? Because the motion of placing the wire on a hot piece of metal is more difficult and delicate than

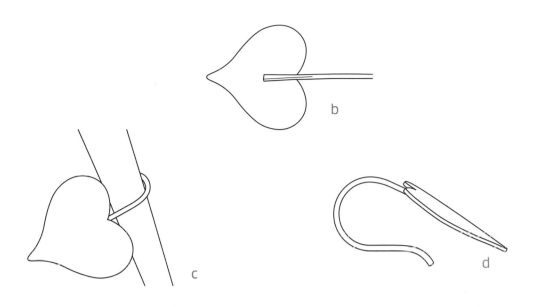

b

c

d

that of moving a torch around, so you need your steadier hand for this.

7 Grab the locking tweezers in your dominant hand. Heat up the solder with your torch in the other hand. When the solder begins to flow into a pool, gently touch the flat part of the wire so the wire will stick straight out of the V. Hold it there for a second, and then quickly remove your torch. Wait a few moments for the solder to "set," and then quench the earring. Pickle as usual and repeat with the second earring. {b}

TIP Because you are using your nondominant hand to hold the torch, and it is probably shaking a bit, the wire will sometimes stealthily scoot to the side and attach crookedly. Should this be the case, simply re-flux the solder, heat, and using your tweezers, lift off the wire when the solder melts. Then start again. There's probably no reason to add more solder, but be sure to pickle the piece in between the soldering attempts.

8 Gently polish the heart with your rouge buff and rouge, being very careful to not hit and warp the wire. If you'd like a matte finish, scrub with the Scotch-Brite pad. The earring needs to be perfect before we shape the ear wire in the last step.

Shape the Ear Wires

9 There should be a length of about 2" (5cm) or more of wire extending from the earring for you to work with. Begin by curving the wire to the back around your pen about ⅜" (9.5mm) up from the heart. Continue until you have a nice U and the wire hangs down in back parallel to the earring. {c} Now cut it to an appropriate length from the top—I usually opt for about ¾" (2cm). Carefully use the rubber wheel in your Dremel to smooth the end so it does not hurt when you put it in your ear. Now take your chain nose pliers and make a little upward bend at the end of the wire, just as you've seen in almost every earring wire out there. {d} You can now do a final buff *carefully* with the Dremel and rouge (although do not bother if you are doing a matte finish), or you can play it safe and just use a polishing cloth.

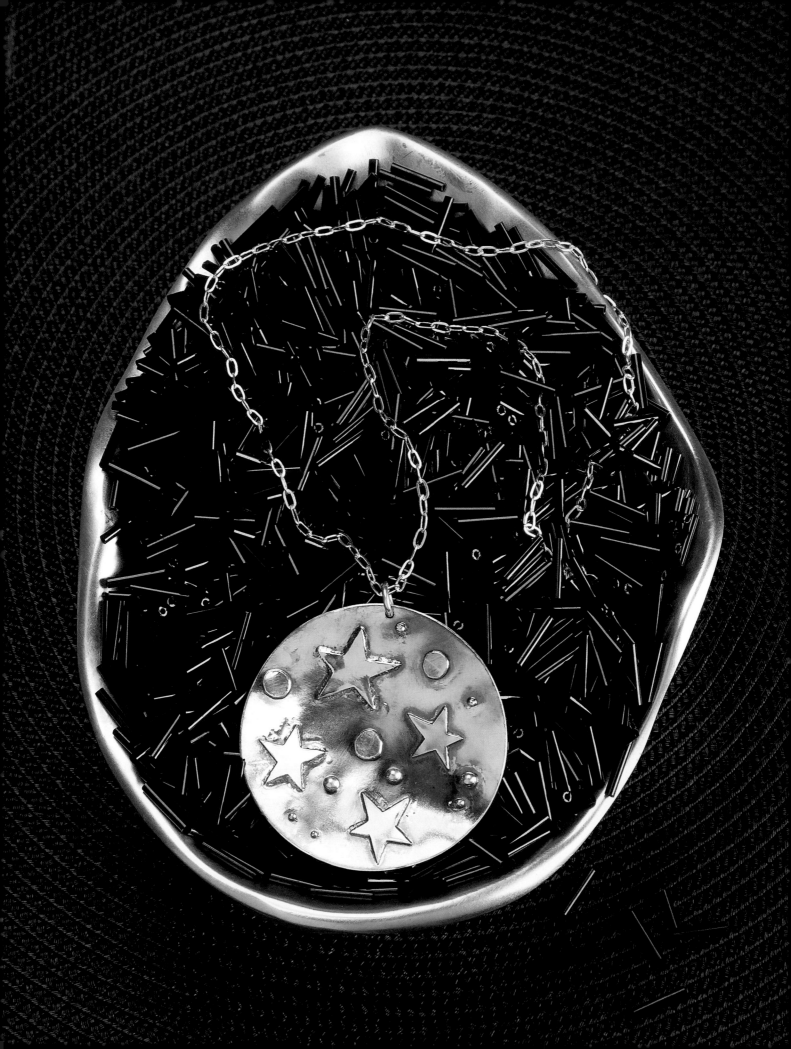

starry night pendant

This pendant was inspired by the sky at night, with its sparkling stars and tiny gemlike planets. What better muse than the night sky? This piece is more or less a literal translation of what I see when I look up at night, with brass "stars" and "planets" set into a sheet of metal. Although you have made a couple of pendants already, this one has a distinctly rough, artistic look. And in making it, I introduce you to another indispensable soldering technique)—"sweat soldering."

This technique has nothing to do with sweating the copper piping under your sink. Rather, you are connecting two pieces so they stack on top of each other. You melt solder into a pool on the top piece and then reheat it to attach the bottom piece. This project invites you to make good use of all the little balls you made in your initial foray into soldering (page 88).

ADVANCED INTERMEDIATE

2" x 2" (5cm x 5cm) sheet 20g sterling silver

2" x 2" (5cm x 5cm) sheet 24g copper or brass

Premade jump ring or 1" (2.5cm) 20g sterling silver wire

Graph paper, pencil, and scissors

Glue stick

Shot made when practicing soldering

Beeswax, soap, or candle

Saw frame and blades

File

Hammer (optional at this point)

Charcoal block and heat-resistant surface like a ceramic dinner plate or metal baking pan

Mini torch

Flux and paintbrush

Shears

Sheet of medium solder

Sheet of easy solder

AA tweezers

Pickle and copper tongs

Tea ball

Center punch and hammer

Drill bit

Dremel with blue rubber wheel, tripoli buff, and rouge buff

Premade sterling silver chain

Design and Cut Out the Shapes

1 Begin by deciding what shape you'd like your pendant to be. I chose to make a round pendant with a 2" (5cm) diameter, but it can be anything. Draw a design on graph paper and cut it out (or use the templates on page 153). Coat the template with the glue stick and affix to the metal. Let dry for 5 minutes. Lubricate your saw

blade with beeswax, soap, or a candle, and saw out the design. File to shape and remove the template.

2 Using your graph paper, make paper models of stars to adorn your pendant. They can be any size. Scrub the brass or copper sheet, dry, and affix the models with the glue stick as above. Saw them out and file to shape.

3 If you have not already, put the little balls you made in the introduction to soldering (page 88) into a tea ball and pickle them. If they are already clean, inspect them for regularity and size. Choose a few that look nice and are somewhat flat on the bottom, and set them aside. If you need to make more with the remnants of your sterling or copper/brass sheet, do so now, referring to the soldering introduction (page 88). You can alter the height of the balls, if you wish, by hammering a few of them flatter. Exercise caution when using the hammer—these balls are very small!

4 Lay out all the elements of your pendant in front of you and draw the design you'd like on a sheet of paper. You will refer to this while assembling the piece. Cut some tiny chips of medium solder and set them aside.

Solder

5 Get out your charcoal block and heat-resistant surface. Place the first star on the

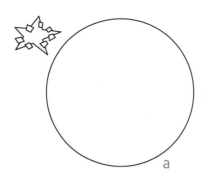

charcoal, flux the *entire* surface, and dry the flux with your flame. Place a few small pieces of solder on the star, being sure to cover the whole piece. Now light your torch and heat up the metal from the top to melt the solder into a pool. Quench. If the metal looks excessively dirty, pickle it. {a}

6 Remove the piece from the pickle, wash with soap and water, and dry. Place the pendant on your charcoal. Now flux the area on which you wish to place the star with the pool of solder and dry it with your torch. Use your tweezers to carefully place the star on top of the pendant. Carefully reheat your star from the top until the solder starts to flow and you see the star sink down into the pendant. Remove your flame and quench. Pickle if necessary. Repeat this technique with the other stars and balls, using medium solder each time. {b} Pickle, wash with soap and water, and dry. Insert the rubber wheel in your Dremel and polish the pendant.

7 Use the center punch and hammer to make a divot at the top of the pendant for a hole at the top of the pendant for your bail. Insert the drill bit in the Dremel and drill the hole. Use a premade jump ring or create one from your 20g wire, thread it through the hole, and solder it closed as in step 8 of the ID Bracelet (page 108). Polish with tripoli and rouge. Wash well, dry and slip onto a chain.

four

the ring mandrel and bezel burnisher

Rings are my favorite pieces of jewelry to make. They are the most powerful, with the most symbolism attached)—high school ring, wedding ring, baby ring, anniversary ring, I-just-got-a-promotion ring. And since they're often worn continuously, they can become an integral part of one's persona and look. This chapter introduces two industry-specific tools—a mandrel for forming rings and a burnisher for setting stones. Now your imagination can *really* run wild!

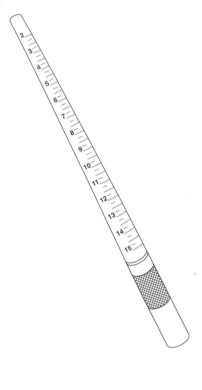

Ring Mandrel

A jeweler's mandrel is simply a graduated taper made of stainless steel, often with ring sizes marked on it, that is used to form perfect circles out of metal. It is used by wrapping metal—sheet or wire—around it with your fingers or with a hammer. Think of it as a larger version of the pen or chopstick you may have used to make jump rings, like in the ID Bracelet (page 106). The mandrel is a heavy number and tends to roll if not anchored down or stored vertically. Be careful where you place it when not in use, or you risk smashing fingers and toes.

Use a mandrel as a simple prop around which to wrap wire or sheet to make circles. Like your frozen juice can, it can be used flat on the bench, or held in your hand while you twirl wire around it.

Burnisher

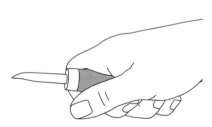

A burnisher is a short, curved, and smooth stainless steel blade with a wooden handle. *Burnishing* simply means making a surface smooth by rubbing it and, for our purposes, will be used only for stone setting. Once you have made a bezel setting for your stone—more on that later—you will use the burnisher to push the bezel around the stone to secure it.

A burnisher is held in your fist in a way similar to how you eat a giant turkey leg—just sort of grabbing it and munching away. You're doing the same thing here, minus the chow-down. You will largely use the burnisher in an apple-peeling motion, bringing the blade toward you in a curling down motion. Think of moving your hand from a palm-forward position to a palm-facing-down position by bending your wrist towards you. It's the same motion you use when you rev the throttle on a motorcycle. You brace your thumb on the bezel to anchor your hand. (This is much simpler than it sounds and will make sense when we begin a project.)

Stones

One of the most exciting parts of jewelry making is designing a piece with a beautiful stone. There is a dizzying array of stones out there, but for now let's keep it simple. You are going to be working with cabochon-cut stones in semiprecious gems. What the heck is a cabochon? A cabochon (or *cab*) is a stone cut so that it is flat on the bottom and domed on top. Cabs come in all different shapes, colors, and sizes. It's so much fun to shop at a gem store and choose. For now, however, limit yourself to working with round and oval cabs. They are the easiest and most foolproof to set, perfect for the novice.

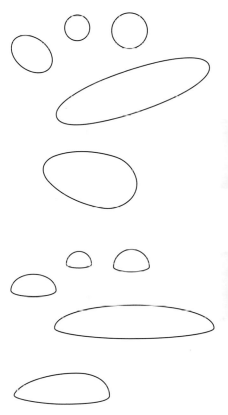

As with any other technique I introduce in this book, I like to start big. In class, I have my students buy stones that are at least 10mm in a round or oval shape. It's difficult to make a bezel for a tiny stone the first time out, and I like to err on the side of success, not frustration. Once you have mastered setting a larger stone, go as small as you like.

While cabs are cut in many varieties of gemstones, I suggest starting with inexpensive stones, such as onyx, amethyst, or tiger-eye; with anything from the quartz family, such as rose quartz, smoky topaz; or with malachite or turquoise. Stay away from precious aquamarines and opals for now—they are quite expensive and very fragile. I always ask my beginners to buy relatively inexpensive stones: In fact, my supply sheet yells out, "Do not spend more than five dollars on your first stone!" Fortunately, five dollars gets you a lot of stones if you go to the right sources, many of which I list on page 154. You will be shocked at how little some stones can cost—literally fifty cents or less at times! When you do shop for stones, whether it's in a catalog or at a store, buy several in different shapes and colors so that you will have a nice variety to work with.

hammered band ring

A chunky ring looks great and always garners compliments. For your first foray into using a ring mandrel, we'll make a simple, thick band ring that you can texture as you please. The nice thing about this ring is that there are endless variations. They are perfect for both men and women. Kids (and their parents) like them because they are relatively injury resistant (kids + prong-set diamond = um, no).

Make one in gold, and you have a classic wedding band. You can make thin ones to stack, a super-thick version to wear on your thumb, or one somewhere in between. You can even make one with thick wire. Once you get the hang of making a plain band ring, you can begin flexing your artistic muscles by making one with cutout shapes, one with wavy edges, one that is thick in front and thin in back . . . the possibilities are limitless! Rings like this are democratic: Any metal looks good. And they look good on anyone. I made one of mine with a traditional hammered texture, but the cool "bark" texture on my wide ring was created by scratching the surface with a scribe made from a coat hanger and then polishing it.

INTERMEDIATE

1" x 4" (2.5cm x 10cm) 20g sterling, copper, or brass sheet

Sheet of graph paper, pencil, and scissors

Ruler

Permanent marker

Beeswax, soap, or candle

Saw frame and blades

File

Ring mandrel

Hammer

Charcoal block and heat-resistant surface like a ceramic dinner plate or metal baking pan

Mini torch

Flux and paintbrush

Shears

Sheet of easy solder

Locking tweezers with a weighted base

AA tweezers

Pickle and copper tongs

Dremel with blue rubber wheel, tripoli buff, and rouge buff

Sheets of sandpaper in 320–600 grit

Tripoli

Rouge

Scribe made from a coat hanger (to use to create a "bark" texture)

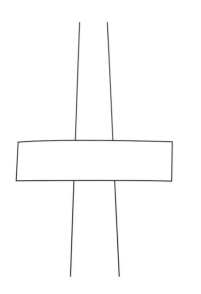

a

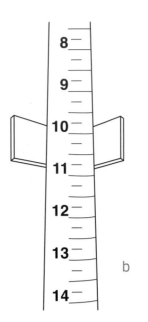

b

Cut Out the Band

1 First, determine your ring size. Now, as with most things in jewelry, there are mathematical ways of doing this, but for my money, the best way for a beginner to size a ring is to make a paper template. Simply cut a strip of graph paper in a width that is appealing to you and wrap it around the knuckle of the finger you wish to adorn, being sure it will fit over your knuckle. The rings pictured on page 122 are 17mm, 9mm, and 3mm wide, from left to right. Mark your strip at the length you need.

NOTE: If you are making a super-thick band, allow extra length. Remember, the ring has to go over your knuckle, and you can't finesse a thick band over a knuckle like you can with a thin one.

2 When your paper model is ready, place it at one edge of your metal sheet and trace around it. Always line up your template at the edge of the metal, avoiding the necessity to saw *two* sides!

3 Lubricate your saw blade with beeswax, soap, or a candle, and saw out the band. If necessary, file the edges smooth.

Shape the Band

4 Set your mandrel on the edge of your bench and angle it up. Place your band over the middle of the mandrel and press down with your hands. {a} Push it as far as you can, lift up the mandrel, and then hold it vertically. Continue to press the band around it. Finally, lay the mandrel flat on your bench and hammer the two sides together. {b}

5 You will not be able to get the two sides together perfectly around the mandrel. Slide the ring off the mandrel, place it on your bench seam side up, and put your index finger of your nondominant hand *inside* the ring to hold it steady. Now, using your hammer, carefully hammer the two edges together. Don't worry if it's no longer round—you will fix that later. The main object is to make sure the two edges are flush and meet cleanly so they will solder well. If there are gaps at the meeting point, or if one side is crooked, just slide the ring down the mandrel to open it, file the offending area, and hammer them back together. If the metal is impossible to work with, consider annealing it. You want to get the edges as close together and as flat as

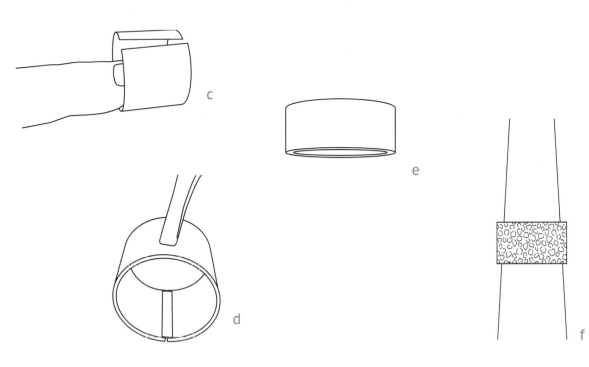

possible, so if this means you have to hammer straight down on the seam, do so. {c}

Solder

6 When the edges are together, anchor the ring upside down in the locking tweezers so the seam is at the bottom, and place the base on your charcoal. If necessary, set the charcoal on one end—you may need the extra height because you will heat the ring with your torch from below. Flux the seam and dry it with your torch. Cut a long, wide strip of easy solder— one that is big enough to completely cover the seam and as long as the ring band is wide. Use tweezers to place it exactly along the seam. {d} Light up the torch and preheat the whole ring. When it's hot, turn your torch upside down, and heat the ring forward and backward from underneath along the seam. The solder will pull down into the seam. Once it does, remove your flame and let the ring air cool. Do not quench! We want to keep the ring annealed from heating it so we can reshape it if necessary. {e}

7 When it is cool, pickle the ring. Wash with soap and dry well, then slide it back on the mandrel and gently hammer it until it's round again, if necessary.

8 Insert the rubber wheel in your Dremel and polish both the surface and the edges of the ring. If the wheel will fit into the interior of the ring, polish along the same as well. Otherwise, use a small sheet of 320-grit sandpaper to smooth the inside, repeating with 400-, 500-, and 600-grit sandpaper until smooth. Use tripoli to polish the ring inside and out. Finally, if texture is desired, use the ball end of your hammer and hammer while the ring is on the mandrel. {f} If you would like to create a bark texture, slide the ring on the mandrel to keep it steady, and etch lines on the ring with the scribe. Do a final polish with rouge, wash well, and dry.

bauble ring

INTERMEDIATE

1" x 4" (2.5cm x 10cm) 20g sterling, copper, or brass sheet

2" (5cm) 20g sterling, copper, or brass wire

1' or more (30.5cm) 22g or 24g sterling, copper, or brass wire—whichever gauge will fit through your beads

Graph paper, pencil, and scissors

Ruler

Permanent marker

Beeswax, soap, or candle

Saw frame and blades

File

Ring mandrel

Hammer

Charcoal block and heat-resistant surface like a ceramic dinner plate or metal baking pan

Flux and paintbrush

Shears

Sheet of hard solder

Sheet of easy solder

Two pairs of locking tweezers

AA tweezers

Round nose pliers

Chain nose pliers

Pickle and copper tongs

Tea ball

Dremel with blue rubber wheel, tripoli buff, and rouge buff

Tripoli

Rouge

Sheets of sandpaper in 320–600 grit

7–8 beads of your choosing (mine were 8mm, 9mm, and 10mm in diameter)

I have sold countless rings based on this design, and it's easy to see why! One part funky cocktail ring and another part toy, it epitomizes "fun" jewelry and appeals to all ages. The variations available in this style are many. I used semi-precious gemstone beads in mine, but plastic, glass, wood, or pretty much any other bead looks great, too. Pearls work as well and lend an "earthy" look.

I use gemstone beads in a faceted rondel shape. A faceted rondel looks like a round bead cut in half and faceted like a diamond. I like this style because it's nearly flat, so it doesn't protrude *too* much, and the facets lend a sparkly touch. You can make the ring in sterling, brass, or copper; with a thin band, with a thick band, with a textured band . . . whatever strikes your fancy. You can, of course, alter the shape or the style of the bead, mix up the colors as I have done, or use more or fewer beads. The beautiful thing about the Bauble Ring is that it's noncommittal. Made one, but hate the bead you chose? Cut it off and try another.

Finally, from a skill standpoint, this ring reinforces the ability to multitask while soldering, which you learned if you made the Heart Earrings (page 110). It also teaches you how to create a ball at the end of a wire so you can make your own head pins for beads. This is a fun technique that you will find indispensable as you continue on your jewelry journey.

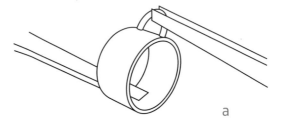

a

b

1 Make a ring in a width and style of your choice following steps 1–8 of the Hammered Band Ring (page 124) but use hard solder instead of easy.

Shape and Solder the Loop

2 Use your round nose pliers to bend the 20g wire into a loop that is about ⅛" (3mm) or more tall and as wide as the width of your ring band. Clip the end with your wire cutters and file both ends perfectly straight.

3 Anchor the ring in your locking tweezers standing upright, with the soldered seam directly in the middle on top. Flux the seam and dry the flux with your torch. Cut 2 rectangular pieces of easy solder about ¹⁄₁₆" (1.5mm) wide. Use your AA tweezers to place them on the seam at each edge of the ring.

4 Place the loop you have just made in your other locking tweezers so that, when it is held, it looks like a rainbow. The "ends" of the rainbow are going to be soldered at the edges of the ring. {a} Place your torch in your nondominant hand, and hold the locking tweezers with the loop in the other. Preheat the ring and then concentrate the flame on the solder. When the solder begins to melt, touch the loop ends to the pool of solder. Immediately pull your flame away and hold the loop still for a moment to let the solder set. Unlock both locking tweezers, quench the ring, and pickle as usual. {b}

Make the Head Pins for the Beads

5 Take the 22g or 24g wire and cut it into lengths of about 1½" (3.8cm). Anchor the

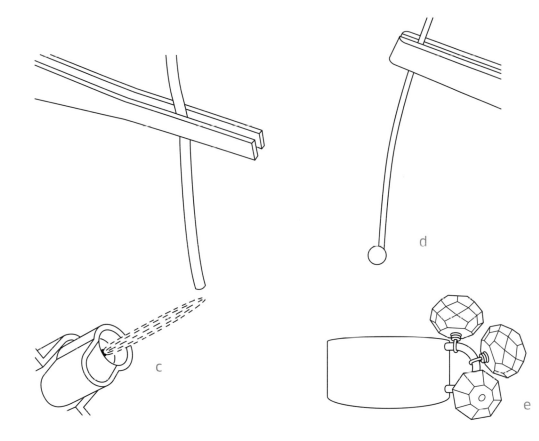

end of one piece in the locking tweezers. Hold it in your dominant hand so it hangs straight down. Light up the torch with the other hand and flip it upside down so the flame points up. {c} Place the flame beneath the hanging end of the wire, and hold it there until you see the wire crawl up and form a ball. Take the flame away and set aside to cool. Do not quench, as we want the metal to remain annealed so it's easy to wrap the beads. {d} If you find this soldering position uncomfortable, you can also heat the end of the wire with your torch from the side. Use the remaining wire to make one head pin for each bead. Place them in your tea ball and pickle.

6 Insert the rubber wheel in the Dremel and polish both the surface and the edges of the ring. If the wheel will fit into the interior of the ring, polish along the same as well. Other-

wise, use a small sheet of 320-grit sandpaper to smooth the inside, repeating with 400-, 500-, and 600-grit sandpaper until smooth. Use tripoli to polish the ring inside and out. Wash well and pat dry, then polish with rouge. Do not use polishing compound once the beads have been attached.

7 Take the head pins out of the pickle, wash with soap and water, and dry well. String a bead onto the first wire and attach it to the loop on the top of the ring. See steps 3–4 on page 28. The only difference is you don't have to make a loop for your bead to rest on—your head pin now does that duty! Don't attach the bead too closely to the ring—you want it to move about. Attach the remainder of the beads. {e}

layered wire ring

So far we have used wire by itself and bent it to our whim to create shapes. But, just like people, a wire sometimes wants to cuddle up with another. This ring is a great example of how to work with wire and get a totally different shape, style, and effect.

Our stacked wire ring has a layered look that transcends trends and eras. As with a band ring, it's timeless and can be endlessly tweaked depending on the style desired. Make it in all sterling or mix up the metals. Alternate the sizes of the wire: I like a thick outer wire that frames the middle ones. Men in particular love this ring if it's made with thicker wire—it has a boxy, masculine look. It can also double as a band for the gemstone ring you will be making soon.

This project is valuable for learning the technique to successfully solder wire together horizontally. Although the premise is easy, it takes a bit of patience to make a nice, smooth seam between the wires. Plus, you get to stick things with pins and release your inner voodoo priestess!

ADVANCED INTERMEDIATE

1' (30.5cm) 14g sterling wire or a mix of sterling, copper, and brass wires

Graph paper, pencil, permanent marker, and scissors, and ruler

Wire cutters

Chain nose pliers

Masking tape

Hammer

Pins

Charcoal block and heat-resistant surface

Mini torch

Flux and paintbrush

Shears

Sheets of easy and medium solder

Sheet of easy solder

AA tweezers

Pickle and copper tongs

File

Beeswax, soap, or candle

Saw frame and saw blades

Ring mandrel

Locking tweezers with weighted base

Dremel with blue rubber wheel, tripoli buff, and rouge buff

Sheets of sandpaper in 320–600 grit

Tripoli and rouge

Create the Band

1 Determine your ring size using a paper model (see step 1 of the Hammered Band Ring on page 124).

Prepare the Wires

2 Straighten the wire using your hands and tape-wrapped chain nose pliers, if needed, and cut the wire into 3 pieces that equal your

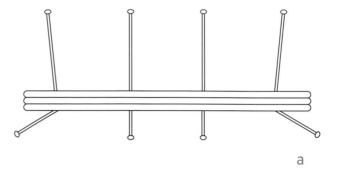

a

ring length *plus* ¼" (6mm). Straighten the wires by holding one flat on your bench and rolling them with your fingers as you would pie dough, while simultaneously gently hammering out kinks. Do this for all 3 wires, line them up, and make sure each wire lines up with its mates perfectly. There can be no gaps between wires when they're lined up. Gaps will lead to globules of solder and ruin the look of the ring.

3 When the wires are perfect, line them up horizontally on your charcoal block. Stick a pin into the charcoal behind the furthest wire, and then insert 3 more so that there are 4 pins evenly spaced. Do the same with 4 more pins on the front wire. The wires will now be in a little pin corral, and thus will not move when you solder. {a}

Solder

4 Flux the entire length of the wires, and dry with your flame. Cut tons of tiny, tiny slivers of medium solder and put them on the edge of your charcoal. They should be minuscule, like the metal filings you get from, well, filing. Use your tweezers to lay the pieces of solder along the gap between each of the wires. Space them out evenly, but do not use too much—the solder will goop up, fill in the channel between the wires, and the ring loses the detail. {b}

5 Light your torch and preheat the piece. Then begin heating one end and move the flame back and forth until the solder there begins to melt; immediately continue to move the flame along the length of the wire. The solder will flow along the way and make a nice line.

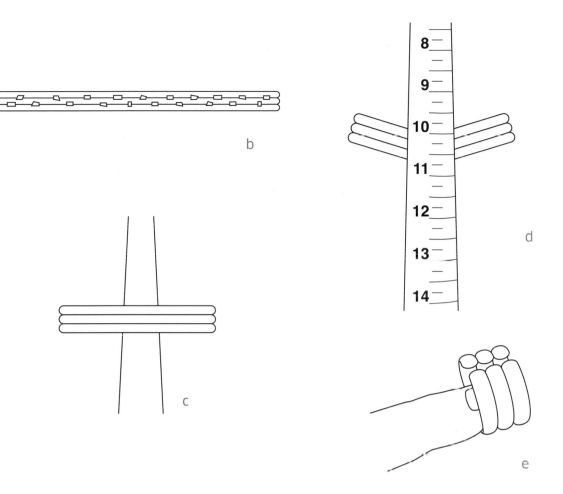

b

c

d

e

Go all the way to the other end and let the piece air cool. Pickle as usual. When done, wash with soap and water and dry. Check the seams of the wires for gaps. If you find any, use a tiny amount of solder to fill.

6 File one end of the band straight. Measure your ring size from the filed end, and saw off the excess length. File this end straight as well.

Shape the Band

7 Wrap the ring around the ring mandrel as in steps 4–6 of the Hammered Band Ring (page 124). File the ends if necessary to make them meet well, and solder as described above. Pickle, wash well, and dry. {c}, {d}, and {e}

8 Slide the ring back on the mandrel and *gently* hammer it until it's round again, if necessary. You do not want to flatten the wires, so go at it carefully.

9 Insert the rubber wheel in the Dremel and *gently* polish the surface of the ring only where necessary. Do not do this aggressively, as you can flatten the wires in places and ruin the look. Do the same with the edges of the ring. If the rubber wheel will fit into the interior of the ring, polish along the same as well. Otherwise, use a small sheet of 320-grit sandpaper to smooth the inside, repeating with 400, 500, and 600 grits until smooth. Use tripoli and then rouge to polish the ring inside and out.

stone pendant necklace

So far you've made plenty of beautiful metal jewelry, and now it's time to enhance all that fabulousness with stones. We are going to begin with cabochon stones, perfect for getting your feet wet. A stone-set pendant is a great way to enter into this new realm because it needs a little more work to fabricate a bezel to hold the stone. You will see what I mean in a moment.

The main point of this project is to learn how to craft a rim—called a bezel—that will hold a stone. It is basically a silver ring that holds the stone in place. You will then solder the bezel to another sheet, called a backplate. Add a bail through which to hang your chain, and you are all set.

I chose the simplest and starkest stone for my pendant—a large oval cabochon in black onyx. Dramatic but simple is the theme here.

ADVANCED INTERMEDIATE

6" x ⅛" (15cm x 3mm) fine silver bezel wire

1" x 1" (2.5cm x 2.5cm) 24g sterling sheet

Cabochon stone of your choosing

Shears

AA tweezers

File

Charcoal block and heat-resistant surface like a ceramic dinner plate or metal baking pan

Mini torch

Flux and paintbrush

Sheet of hard solder

Sheet of medium solder

Locking tweezers with weighted base

Pickle and copper tongs

Jump ring

Dremel with blue rubber wheel, tripoli buff, and rouge buff

Burnisher

Cardboard (optional)

Tripoli

Rouge

19" (48.5cm) premade chain

Create the Bezel

1 Use your shears to trim one end of your bezel wire at a 90-degree angle.

2 If you are using an oval stone, beginning at the middle of the long side, carefully wrap the bezel wire around the stone. If you're using a round stone, start wherever you like. Overlap the ends of the bezel wire at the meeting point. Be sure that there is a small triangle of space between the wire and the stone. {a}

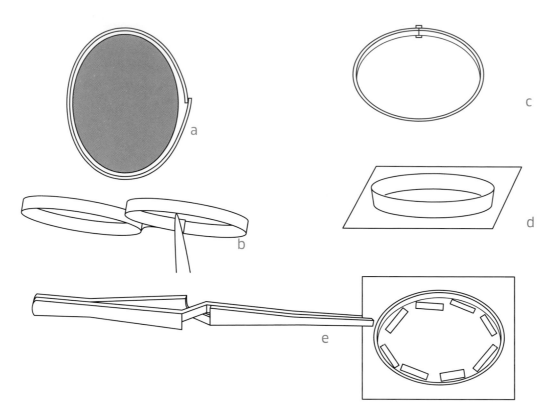

Using tweezers, grasp the wire where the two ends meet and hold. Transfer the tweezers to your nondominant hand, and carefully snip through both wires just to the side of the tweezers. {b}

File the ends of the bezel wire so both are straight. Now check the fit of the bezel around the stone.

Solder the Bezel

To solder, the two ends of the bezel must meet perfectly and stay together on their own. Carefully open and close the ends so that they stay together. If the metal seems stiff and uncooperative, anneal it (page 88).

NOTE: Fine silver will not darken like sterling. Heat only until you see a faint orange glow on the metal. More than this will melt the metal.

Place your bezel on the charcoal with the seam in front of you. Cut a sliver of hard solder and position it on the charcoal perpen-

dicular to the seam. Make sure both that the bezel sits on the solder and that that there is only a sliver of solder showing inside the bezel wall. {c} If there is too much solder on the inside, the stone will not fit properly.

Flux the top of the seam. It will run down and coat the rest of the seam, as well as the solder. It is not necessary to dry it with your flame.

Light your torch. Hold the torch in front of your bezel, angling it at a 45-degree angle to the charcoal about ½" (13mm) in front of your piece. It should not touch the bezel directly. Using a smooth motion, move the flame side to side in front of the bezel. The heat will reflect up to the bezel, and you will see the solder crawl up and jump into the seam. Quench in water.

Carefully file off any excess solder along the seam with a file.

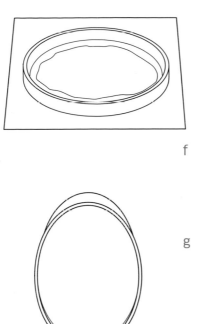

f

g

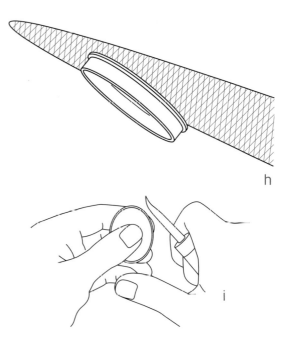

h

i

Prepare and Solder the Backplate

10 For the backplate, use your shears to cut a piece of 24g metal into a square shape that is slightly bigger than your bezel. Flatten it by hammering it gently against your bench if necessary. Place the bezel on it and check to see whether it sits flat. The easiest way to tell is to hold up the piece to the light and see whether any light peeks through the area where the bezel meets the backplate. If it does, gently hammer the backplate some more. {d}

NOTE: If the bezel is a little off, sand it on 220-grit sandpaper until the bottom edge is even.

11 Place the corner of your backplate in the locking tweezers and place on your charcoal. If necessary, set the charcoal on one end—you may need the extra height because you will heat the backplate with your torch from below. Place the bezel in the center of the backplate. Paint the backplate *with the bezel on it* with flux and dry it with your flame. Then cut slivers of medium solder and place them evenly spaced around the inner edge of the bezel flat on the backplate. They should be pressed up against the wall of the bezel. {e}

12 Light up your torch, preheat the piece from the top, turn your torch upside down, and then heat from beneath. Move your torch in a circle that is slightly bigger than the bezel. Solder goes toward the heat, and we want the solder on the *inside* of the bezel to pull through to the *outside*. The solder will begin to melt and swish around the edge of the bezel. Look for a silver line all around the base of the bezel—when you see it all around, you're done. {f}

13 Quench your piece and pickle. Wash with soap and water and dry well.

14 Carefully use your shears to cut around the bezel as close as you are comfortable, but leave a small tab of backplate at the

IF THESE STONES COULD TALK . . .

When thinking about jewelry with stones, it's best to buy the stone first and design your piece around it. It sounds silly, but let the stone "talk" to you and help dictate the design. Also, if you design a piece and then decide to throw a stone into it, you may struggle to find a stone that fits or looks perfect. As most of us know from life experience, poor planning will always end up in frustration. Eliminate frustration from your jewelry life by taking the time to fully design a piece before executing it, particularly when stones are involved.

top of your stone so you can affix a ring—your bail—to attach the pendant to a chain. {g}

15 Now use a file to remove excess backplate around your bezel *except* where your bail will be. When you are done, your bezel and backplate should look like a shallow cup, with no seam visible. {h}

16 Carefully file down the area on the backplate for the bail until it's barely a half circle above your bezel. You want just enough of the backplate left to drill a hole for a jump ring. {g} Drill hole, insert the jump ring, and solder shut. Smooth the entire edge of the bezel and pendant with the rubber wheel inserted in the Dremel. Polish with tripoli and rouge.

Set the Stone

17 Now cut a few pieces of thin cardboard in the same shape as your stone but slightly smaller than it. They need to sit flat in your backplate within the bezel. You may or may not need them, depending on how tall your stone is. Place the stone in your bezel and admire how it looks! Make sure it's not sitting too low, which can look sloppy. You want a nice, high dome, but not so high that you are not able to bend the edges of the bezel over the stone to hold it in place. Add a piece of cardboard under the stone if it does sit too low.

18 Once the stone is in its new home, hold your pendant in your nondominant hand and place your thumb on top of the stone. Using the burnisher, press in the bezel at four places: north, south, east, and west. This ensures that the stone is in place and tacked in. Then, use the burnisher to make an up-and-over motion all around the bezel, and begin pressing the bezel up and over your stone, going all the way around. Be sure to start near the bottom of the bezel up and go all the way up and over the top. Repeat until there are no gaps between the bezel and the stone. {i}

19 Finally, using your burnisher again, hold it as you would hold a potato peeler, and, using a peeling motion, pull it along the top edge of the bezel against the stone. It should leave a nice shiny line. This seals the bezel down over the stone.

20 Polish the bezel again with tripoli and rouge if there are lots of scratches from using the burnisher making sure to avoid the stone. Wait for the compliments!

pendant with tube bail

I made a bail for this pendant, which fetures a yummy stone called a guacamole agate, using part of the backplate and curving it into a tube through which you string a chain. It's easier than it sounds.

MATERIALS USED FOR THE STONE PENDANT NECKLACE PLUS

Round nose pliers

1   Make a bezel and solder it to a backplate as in steps 1–15 of the Stone Pendant Necklace on page 135. However, instead of leaving just a small curved area at the top of your back-plate, leave a larger and longer tab, about ½" to ¾" (13mm–2cm). When done polishing, simply use round nose pliers to curl the tab over and toward the front of the bezel to create a tube. If marks have been made from this step, polish with the rubber wheel and tripoli, if necessary. Then set stone and polish the pendant as in steps 17–20 of the Stone Pendant Necklace (opposite).

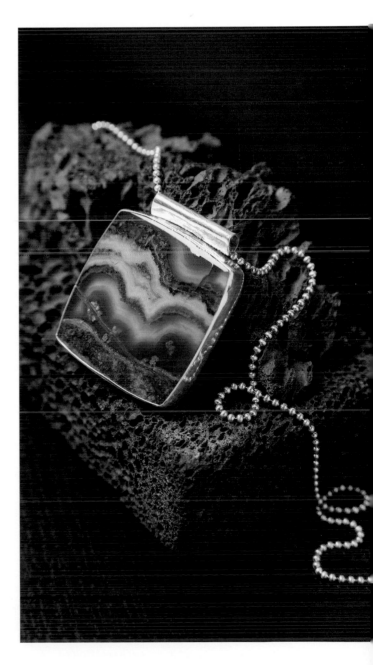

ring with backplated stone

As you know, I love the ring. It's my favorite style of jewelry to make, and, honestly, when free from having to design for a commercial line or commission, I make gigantic, nearly unwearable rings with huge stones. The bigger the stone, the better; the crazier the design, the more I like it. When I teach my beginning students the basics of metalsmithing, I always start by making a ring set with a stone. And everyone is always psyched to finish it and wear it out of class with pride. Half will come back the next week and tell me that their friends are already asking them to make one. What is it about a simple ring with a stone?

If you made the Stone Pendant Necklace (page 134), you thought inexpensive and big for your pendant; modify that thinking just a bit, but stick with the inexpensive part. I recommend using a medium-size cabochon measuring between 8mm and 14mm for now, even if you crave a truly demure ring. Creating bezels for the little stones will drive you mad—at least until you have a few under your belt. So resist the temptation to bite off more than you can chew and focus on making a good-sized ring. You can always give it away if it's truly not *you*.

INTERMEDIATE

6" x ⅛" (15cm x 3mm) bezel wire

1" x 1" (2.5cm x 2.5cm) 24g sterling sheet

1" x 4" (2.5cm x 10cm) 20g sterling, brass, or copper sheet

Graph paper, pencil, permanent marker, and scissors

Cabochon stone of your choosing

Shears

AA tweezers

File

Hammer

Ring mandrel

Beeswax, soap, or candle

Saw frame and blades

Charcoal block and heat-resistant surface like a ceramic dinner plate or metal baking pan

Mini torch

Flux and paintbrush

Sheet of hard solder

Sheet of medium solder

Sheet of easy solder

Locking tweezers with weighted base

Pickle and copper tongs

Sheet of 150-grit sandpaper

Dremel with blue rubber wheel, tripoli buff, and rouge buff

Burnisher

Cardboard (optional)

Tripoli

Rouge

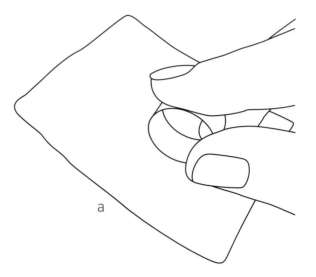

a

Create the Bezel

1 Create a bezel setting on a backplate as in steps 1–16 of the Stone Pendant Necklace (page 135). However, instead of leaving a tab for a bail while filing, file off the all the excess backplate. Insert the rubber wheel in your Dremel and smooth any scratches.

Prepare the Band

2 Measure a ring band using a paper model (see step 1 of the Hammered Band Ring on page 124). Rather than simply going with the same width of rings you've previously made, look at your stone and gauge what width of band would look good with it. Then cut your metal and create the ring described in steps 1–7 of the Hammered Band Ring.

3 Now it's time to sand down the ring band to make a flat area on which to attach the bezel. Hold your ring with the seam down, between the thumb and the index finger in your dominant hand. Press the ring firmly against the sandpaper and push forward, holding it very steady. The object is to create a flat area on the seam, so do your best not to wobble your hand at all. Make a forward push, pick up the ring, move your hand back, and do it again. Do not saw back and forth—you will not have any control, and you may replicate the curve of the ring of which you wish to rid yourself! Make sure your bezel is handy, and check how the band sits on it by putting the ring, seam-side down, on the back of the bezel so it is horizontal to you. *It should stand straight up by itself.* If it doesn't, continue to sand until it does. Do not worry if the ring seems to be getting very thin at the seam: This portion is hidden under the bezel, so it doesn't matter. {a}

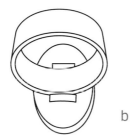

b

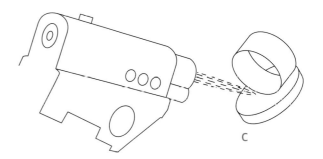

c

NOTE There are two reasons for sanding the ring band before attaching the bezel: 1) As you may have learned in butt soldering the rings for the Cross Earrings (page 102), when soldering, it's always better to join two flush surfaces rather than two surfaces that don't meet well; and 2) if we were to simply solder the bezel onto the rounded ring, it would leave a large space between the two pieces that will catch on your pocket when you put your hand in. It will tear out hair when you run your ringed finger through it. So get out your sheet of 150-grit sandpaper, and get comfortable at your bench.

Solder

4 Place your bezel upside down on your charcoal. Place the ring band with the flattened side down exactly in the middle of the bezel. If it really won't stand up by itself, you can anchor the band in locking tweezers with a weighted base. However, if you have sanded properly, you will not need to. Flux the back of the bezel *with the ring band on it* and dry with your torch. Cut 2 small strips of easy solder and place them horizontally on each side *and* pushed up against the ring band. {b} Preheat your piece and then aim your flame down on the seam of the ring band. Move the flame back and forth within the ring band. You will see the solder flow and go under the band. When it does, take your flame away. Quench and pickle. {c}

Set the Stone

5 Polish the ring with tripoli and rouge, and set the stone as described in steps 17–20 of the Stone Pendant Necklace (page 138). Now tell your friends to get in line for their own. . . .

ring with set-in stone

This project needs no introduction: It's another ring set with a stone, just like the Ring with Backplated Stone on page 140, but in this one the stone sits *directly on* the ring band. Instead of working with premade bezel wire, however, you will fabricate your own bezel wire from a sheet of silver, you will use your ring mandrel in a new and interesting way, and you will use a smaller stone—think 6mm or smaller.

ADVANCED INTERMEDIATE

2" x ½" (5cm x 13mm) 26g sterling silver sheet

1" x 4" (2.5cm x 10cm) 20g sterling, brass, or copper sheet

Graph paper, pencil, permanent marker, and scissors

Cabochon stone of your choosing

Shears

AA tweezers

File

Hammer

Ring mandrel

Sheet of 220-grit sandpaper

Masking tape

Locking tweezers and weighted base

Charcoal block and heat-resistant surface like a ceramic dinner plate or metal baking pan

Mini torch

Flux and paintbrush

Sheet of hard solder

Sheet of medium solder

Sheet of easy solder

Pickle and copper tongs

Dremel with blue rubber wheel, tripoli buff, and rouge buff

Tripoli

Rouge

Burnisher

Cardboard (optional)

Make the Bezel

1 Measure your stone from top to bottom, adding on 2mm to the height. Take this measurement and mark it on the corner of the sheet of 26g sterling. Then mark 2" (5cm) from the corner to form a long strip, and use your shears to cut the strip. It should look like tall bezel wire, which is what it is.

2 Make a bezel as in steps 1–9 of the Stone Pendant Necklace (page 135) but use medium solder instead. It'll feel a little weird, as the bezel is much taller than what you are used to. Do it anyway.

NOTE You are making only a bezel for this ring—no backplate needed!

Make the Band

3 Measure the width of the bezel. Your ring band must be as wide as or even wider than the bezel because the stone needs to sit on the band and not hang over the edge. Determine your ring size, and make a ring band (see steps 1–7 the Hammered Band Ring, page 124) but use hard solder instead of easy.

Curve the Bezel

4 You now need to curve the bottom of the bezel to match the curve of the ring band so that it will sit flush on it. Slide the ring onto your mandrel and note where it sits (usually a mandrel is inscribed with ring sizes, making it easy; otherwise, just make a mental note or mark the mandrel with a permanent marker where your ring fits). Cut a rectangular piece of 220-grit sandpaper about 6" long (15cm), and wrap it tightly around the mandrel where your stone fits. Tape the top and bottom edges with masking tape so it is tight and secure. {a}

5 Angle the mandrel against your bench vertically. Hold your bezel gently by the sides and sand it on the mandrel in an up-and-down motion. {b} Be sure to keep your hand steady and *always hold the bezel in the same direction*. If you like, mark the top of the bezel with a permanent marker so you can be sure you're always holding it the same way. Check the bezel against the ring every 10–15 strokes, and rotate it 180 degrees every once in a while so that the curve you are creating is even on both sides. You need to rotate the bezel because the mandrel is tapered, and one side will end up with a curve that is different from that of the other side. As you continue to sand, you should see that the bezel begins to fit closer and closer to the ring band. {c} And you can now see why you made your bezel so tall. When the bezel sits perfectly on the band, with no gaps, it is ready to be soldered. Check it for height with your stone. If it's too tall, simply turn it upside down and sand down the top on the remaining sheet of sandpaper until the correct height is achieved.

Solder

6 Place the ring in the locking tweezers so that it's held vertically with the seam facing up. Place the bezel on the ring band *on top of the seam*. Flux inside the bezel and dry with your torch. Cut small rectangular slivers of medium solder, and place them all the way around the inside edge of the bezel, being sure that they sit

CREATING A LOGO

By now, you have sawed, filed, formed, soldered, and set stones to your heart's content. You now have a beautiful jewelry collection . . . and as soon as you wear your pieces, someone will want to buy them. What a good problem to have! If you're thinking about developing your own line of jewelry, create a logo to mark your pieces as uniquely yours. I recommend that you buy a custom metal jewelry stamp that you use with the flat side of your hammer to imprint your logo directly into your piece. This is easier than it may sound: Simply design (or have someone design) a logo you like. It can be as simple as your initials to start. Save the design as an Adobe Illustrator or Photoshop file, and bring it to your local jewelry supply store (or email it—see my online supply resources on page 154). They will custom-make a stamp for you, costing between $75 and $200, depending on the complexity of the design. If you make a lot of rings, you will want to get a "gooseneck" stamp that can fit inside the ring to mark it. Otherwise, get a straight stamp. Keep in mind that a jewelry stamp can accommodate a design measuring 3–4mm long, so err on the side of clarity rather than detail when you design your logo.

If nothing else, I suggest that you mark your sterling silver pieces with what's called a *fineness stamp* that indicates the metal content. You will use a "925," "ster," or "sterling" stamp. These can be found at any jewelry supply company.

flat on the ring band and are pushed up against the wall of the bezel as in step 11 on page 137. Light your torch, preheat the ring, flip your torch upside down, and then heat under the bezel until the solder flows. Quench and pickle. When done, wash with soap and water, dry, and polish first with your rubber wheel and then with tripoli and rouge. {d}

7 In a perfect world, a stone on a band could be set just as easily as a stone on a back-plate, but we have a curve to contend with. If your stone is lopsided in its setting, the easiest thing to do is to cut a doughnut shape out of cardboard that sits perfectly within the bezel and up against the wall. Since there's a hole in the middle, this donut will fill in the curve and create a flat area on the ring band. You may need a couple of cardboard donuts. Check the fit of your stone, and when good, set it and polish again as described in steps 17–20 in the Stone Pendant Necklace on page 138.

earrings with stones

These stone-set earrings bring together a lot of the skills we've worked so hard to master, such as jump rings, bezel making, stone setting, and wire forming with a ring mandrel. And more importantly, they're just plain pretty. This pair features three baby cabochon stones cascading from a simple, oversize ear wire. I chose to use translucent amethyst, citrine, and peridot stones because I love the way the light shines through them (and, in fact, in this project you'll learn just *how* to maximize that glow). By graduating the sizes, I brought a delicacy to the form of the earrings. The oversize wires add a modern touch. My stones are 7mm, 6mm, and 4mm, but alter the stone colors and sizes to fit your style.

INTERMEDIATE

1' × ⅛" (30.5cm x 3mm) (or shorter) bezel wire

2" x 2" (5cm x 5cm) 24g sterling sheet

1' (30.5cm) 22g sterling wire

6 cabochon stones of your choosing (3 for each ear)

Shears

Round nose pliers

Chain nose pliers

AA tweezers

File

Hammer

Charcoal block and heat-resistant surface like a ceramic dinner plate or metal baking pan

Mini torch

Flux and paintbrush

Sheet of hard solder

Sheet of medium solder

Sheet of easy solder

Pickle and copper tongs

220-grit sandpaper

Tea ball

Drill bit

Dremel with blue rubber wheel, tripoli buff, and rouge buff

Tripoli

Rouge

Burnisher

Cardboard (optional)

Ring mandrel

Create the Bezels and Bezel Loops

1 Create a bezel setting for each stone on a backplate as in steps 1–13 of the Stone Pendant Necklace project on page 135. {a} Do not trim off the excess backplate!

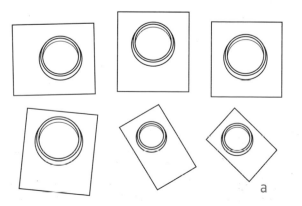

a

b

c

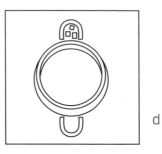

d

2 Cut a ½" (13mm) piece of 22g wire and bend it around the very tip of your round nose pliers to make an open loop. {b} Snip it off with your shears and, holding it carefully, file the two ends flat. It should look like a little C. {c} Repeat this to make a total of 10 loops. Place them on your bench and check them to be sure they lie flat. If not, correct this by gently pinching them between chain nose pliers or hammering them gently.

Solder

3 You now need to solder the loops onto the backplates at the top and bottom of your bezels. Begin with the bezel for the top stone, and flux at the area of the backplate at the seam of the bezel. Dry with your torch. Cut a tiny piece of medium solder, small enough to fit inside the C you've just made. Place the C on the backplate over the seam and push it up against the bezel so it's against the seam of the bezel. Be sure the C is touching the bezel, or it will not look neat. Place the piece of medium solder in the middle of the C. {d}

4 Light up your torch and preheat the whole piece. Then hold your torch parallel to and about 1" (2.5cm) away from the backplate, and move it around the C. Don't get too close! The wire is quite thin and can melt. Heat until

the solder melts and immediately remove your flame. Quench. Now do this with the opposite C, making sure they are exactly opposite. Repeat to add loops for the middle bezels. Place all 4 bezels in the tea ball and pickle.

5 Repeat the steps above for the bottom bezels, but add just 1 loop instead of 2.

6 Insert a drill bit in the Dremel and drill out the middle of every loop.

7 File and polish all 6 bezels (see steps 14–16 of Pendant Set with Stone). If necessary, fold a piece of 220-grit sandpaper and use the edge to get into the tight area between the loop and bezel. Be sure that the bezels look perfect now—this piece is delicate, and you don't want to be forced to do a lot of polishing once it's assembled.

Make and Attach Jump Rings

8 Using your round nose pliers again, make 4 jump rings by wrapping the 22g wire around the tip of the pliers to make a little coil. Slide off the pliers and cut through to make 4 rings. File the edges smooth.

9 Slip an open jump ring into 1 loop on the bezel for the top stone, and then slip on the bezel for the middle stone. Close the jump ring.

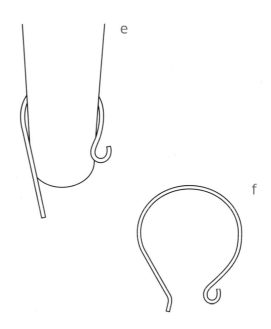

10 Solder the jump ring closed as described in steps 6–8 of the ID Bracelet (page 106). Repeat this step for the jump ring connecting the middle and bottom stones.

Set the Stones

11 Carefully polish the earrings with tripoli. Wash well with soap and water and dry. If necessary, cut a few tiny pieces of cardboard to bolster your stones. If you are using translucent stones like the ones shown, take a piece of scrap 24g sheet from making your backplate, and polish it up with tripoli so it really shines. Then use your shears to cut from it several round pieces that will fit into the bottom of the bezel(s) for the translucent stone(s). Lining your bezel with a polished piece of sterling makes light reflect up through the stone and shows it off better. You can also use a piece of aluminum foil if you *really* smooth it out, but I find that a little piece of silver is better. Place the silver in the bottom of your bezel *on top of* any cardboard you may use.

12 Set your stones as described in steps 17–20 in the Stone Pendant Necklace project on page 138. It doesn't matter what order you go in . . . they all need to be set!

13 Cut two 1½" (3.8cm) pieces of 22g sterling wire for your ear wires. Using your round nose pliers, create a small loop at one end, and leave it open. Now take your ring mandrel and wrap the wire about 1" (2.5cm) from the tip to form a nice big loop. You could also make an even larger loop—it's your choice. {e} Trim the wire as needed, use a rubber wheel to smooth the end, and give the end of the loop a little curl with the round nose pliers. {f} Gently flatten the middle of the ear wire with your hammer to harden it. Repeat with the other wire. Slip the earring through the ear wire, tighten with pliers, and repeat with the other earring.

templates

Below are templates for some of the projects in *Chic Metal*. To use them, simple trace them onto a sheet of tracing paper and cut out as necessary. Then glue them to your metal using a glue stick or rubber cement, and use them as a guide when you saw the designs. The templates are currently at 100%; reduce or enlarge them to your liking by photocopying them at a smaller or higher percentage. Once you are comfortable working with templates in general, I encourage you to make your own. After all, *Chic Metal* is all about finding your own inner design diva!

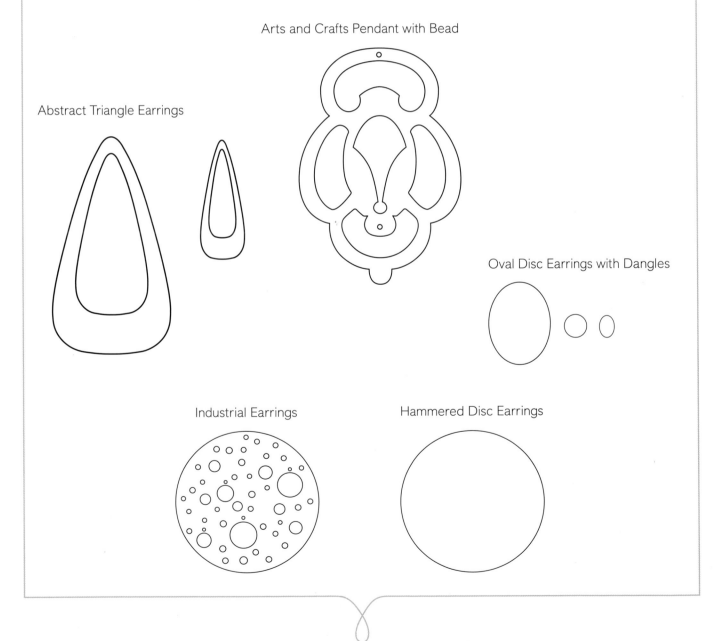

Arts and Crafts Pendant with Bead

Abstract Triangle Earrings

Oval Disc Earrings with Dangles

Industrial Earrings

Hammered Disc Earrings

Chandelier Earrings

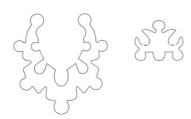

Charm Bracelet

Starry Night Pendant

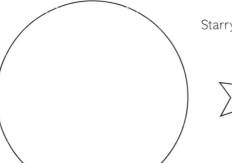

Heart Earrings

Resources

Unlike the supplies used in many other crafts, for which you can often raid your grandmother's attic or kids' arts 'n' crafts area, your *Chic Metal* needs are a little more specific and may seem a bit harder to find. Much as I've been trying to pitch to my local hardware store the value of selling sterling silver sheet and ring mandrels, I have not yet succeeded. I'm obviously too ambitious in my quest to make jewelry supplies mainstream. But fear not! Although metal jewelry-making supplies are a bit more unusual than a skein of yarn, a glue gun, or a bolt of cloth, there are plenty of sources out there for the intrepid jewelry designer.

The list that follows is just the tip of the iceberg, but it will help you find the items you need to complete the projects in this book. I urge you to shop around online, too. eBay.com is an excellent place to look for jewelry-related stuff, even if only to help you figure out what the heck some of the things I'm talking about are. Craigslist.org can be great: Check out the "jewelry" area in "stuff for sale," or list an ad for used jewelry equipment and see who contacts you with what! I love flea markets and garage sales, too, where you can find quirky old machinery and tools. I once bought a bunch of hemostats at a stoop sale to use in lieu of locking tweezers. Not sure that the doctor selling them had soldering in mind, but they work for me! At flea markets, I also round up glass "stones" and drops from vintage decorative lamps, as well as bits of tile you can set like stones, polished pebbles, shells, or old coins. And it goes without saying that there are always tons of vintage and costume jewelry bearing beads to pilfer. Flea markets and garage sales are obviously great places for used furniture. Lesser-known but equally oddball venues for cool stuff are local auctions and estate sales. They aren't just for antiques; you never know what you may find. I almost bought a bunch of lapidary machines at one . . . until I realized I had no space for them, since they themselves were the size of my apartment.

Finally, let's talk about people, the best resource of all. For more industry-specific supplies, an excellent people resource are independent jewelers and teachers of jewelry making in your area, all of whom can make recommendations on where to buy supplies. They can be particularly useful in helping you prioritize your needs in terms of tools and supplies. Local fashion designers will usually have taken at least one jewelry-making course at art school (and they may tell you how that one ring sent them running from metal into the refuge of cloth). Ask them for ideas nonetheless. Check out traditional crafts stores, too. Finally, explore your local hardware store for some of the more routine items I suggest, with an eye to finding alternatives to some of the supplies. As with everything in jewelry making, use your imagination . . . and see what you can find.

Metals, Chains, Findings and Tools

Hauser & Miller

www.hauserandmiller.com

800-462-7447

Another well-known site for metal sheet and wire, known particularly for their fine gold alloys.

Hoover & Strong (metal only)

www.hooverandstrong.com

800-759-9997

A great place for sterling silver sheet, wire, and findings, and one of the oldest and most recognized in the country.

Metalliferous

www.metalliferous.com (mail order or in-store)

212-944-0909

36 West 46th St.

New York, NY 10036

One of New York City's best known and loved jewelry supply stores that carries pretty much everything you need from sterling, copper and brass wire and sheet metal to chains, findings and every tool under the sun. Shop in person or download a catalog from their website and order by mail. Metalliferous sells to many of the most famous jewelry companies in the world, and they ship worldwide . . . and quickly. And, if you're in New York, you can go visit their sister bead store, Beadaliferous, which has a fun, ever-changing selection.

Monsterslayer (metal only)

www.monsterslayer.com

505-598-5322

Ignore the Dungeons & Dragons name, and bear with the clunky interface. This site has great prices for sterling silver sheet, wire, and findings. In industry-speak, their prices are just a few cents above "spot," meaning the current market price of silver, which the site prominently features on its home page. In fact, if you want to try your hand in the commodities market, you can even check the "spot" price of silver on the site and use their button to calculate the cost of what you want to buy, and then wait a bit to see if you can get it more cheaply . . . or—the downside of day trading—more expensively!

Myron Toback

www.myrontoback.com (mail order or in-store)

800-223-7550

25 West 47th St.

New York, NY 10036

Another NYC fave, these lovely folks stock metal, chains, and findings in sterling silver and gold. But you don't have to be in NY to order from them: like Metalliferous, just download a catalog from their website and order by mail.

Rio Grande (mail order only)

www.riogrande.com (mail order only)

800-545-6566

Your one-stop shop. Mail order only, so call to request a catalog, then be blown away by the offerings! This is a great source for everything from tools to metals to pre-made findings to . . . whatever else you can think of that's related to jewelry.

Gemstones and Beads

Artbeads

www.artbeads.com (internet only)

866-715-BEAD

A dizzying selection of beads and beading needs.

Fire Mountain Gems

www.firemountaingems.com (internet/mail order)

800-423-2319

Shop from their website or order a catalog and read while in the baths. In addition to a huge assortment of stones and beads, they carry basic jewelry making and beading supplies.

Rio Grande

Find contact information in Metals, Chains, Findings and Tools, above. In addition to being the preeminent site for metal and tools, Rio hosts a huge assortment of gemstones and beads.

Thai Gem

www.thaigem.com (internet only)

66-39-344771

Don't be put off by the international address—these folks stock a huge collection of well-priced stones and deliver as quickly as any domestic company.

Toho Shoji

www.tohoshoji-ny.com (internet only)

212-868-7465

A great site with a wonderful array of beads and beading supplies.

Trimmings

While fabric trimming stores may sound odd as sources for making metal jewelry, they often have interesting buttons and other elements that can be used in the place of stones, for example. Of course, you can also get cool beads here, as well as chain, hardware (should you be inspired to make a keychain or belt), and lots of things you never knew you needed for jewelry . . . until now!

Botani Trimmings

www.botaniusa.com

212-244-3222

M&J Trimmings

www.mjtrim.com

800-9-MJTRIM

Trim Fabric

www.trimfabric.com

info@trimfabric.com

General Arts and Crafts Supplies

Amazon

www.amazon.com

eBay

www.eBay.com

Google Product Search

www.google.com/products

Jo-Ann Fabric and Craft Stores

www.joann.com

888-739-4120

Michaels

www.michaels.com

800-MICHAELS

Pearl Paint

www.pearlpaint.com

800-451-PEARL

Hardware

Kmart

www.kmart.com

866-KMART-4U

Lowe's

www.lowes.com

800-445-6937

Sears

www.sears.com

800-349-4358

Target

www.target.com

800-591-3869

The Home Depot

www.homedepot.com

800-553-3199

Walmart

www.walmart.com

800-WAL-MART

glossary of terms

Anneal A process in which you heat a piece of metal so that is becomes more pliable and easier to manipulate. The scientific reason for this is that heating the metal spreads the molecules. But just think of it as a specific way of heating metal to make it easier to work with.

Backplate The sheet of metal onto which a bezel is soldered. Can also just mean the backing to a piece of jewelry.

Bail The loop at the top of a pendant through which a chain is threaded.

Bezel A strip of metal that is formed into the size and shape of a stone and then soldered into place on a piece of jewelry so it holds the stone firmly.

Briolette A bead in a pear, heart, or oval shape with triangular facets like a diamond.

Burnish To make metal smooth by rubbing with a tool, usually called a burnisher.

Cabochon A gemstone shape with a convex top and flat or nearly flat bottom.

Divot A little crater made with a sharp tool to anchor a drill bit when drilling.

Jump rings A round loop that is used to connect elements of a piece.

Scribe A sharp pick used to gently scratch lines into metal to mark lines to saw or indicate general measurements; Used in soldering to move metal and/or solder pieces if necessary.

Oxidation The interaction between oxygen molecules and metals that results in the surface of the metal developing a dark patina.

Paillon Literally, a thin piece of metal, but for jewelers the term refers to a small chip of solder.

Planish A technique in which a hammer is used to smooth metal.

Quench To cool a piece of metal by plunging it into water.

Rondel bead Literally meaning round, a rondel bead looks like a ball that has been compressed a little so it's wider than it is tall.

Shot Tiny metal balls made by overheating pieces of metal sheet or wire.

acknowledgments

You incur many debts in writing a book. Some are tangible, others are not. Writing itself can feel like such an impossibly solitary endeavor, but the reality is that you are supported by a huge community of people. And you owe them a lot. So much for solipsism: Here are just a few people in my community to thank.

Sharon Bowers, agent extraordinaire, who has stuck with me from the very beginning of *Chic Metal*, when it was supposed to be a scholarly book based on my dissertation about social contact theory. How she pulled the brilliant idea of a metal jewelry-making book from a treatise on Enlightenment philosophy, I will never know. But I sure am grateful for it!

David Shupe, husband extraordinaire, who has supported me over the years in more ways that I can express. His unflappable confidence in me has made my dream of becoming a jeweler possible. Thanking him enough? Impossible.

My wonderful Potter Craft editors Jen Graham and Melissa Bonventre, as well as the rest of their talented team, who have brought to life this book with a beauty and fullness that I could never have imagined. I am thrilled and honored to have worked with you.

Dr. Susan Budney. She was a lifesaver three years ago and continues to make my life better. I simply could not have written this book without her support.

David Feldman, dear friend and overall know-it-all, who just plain bailed me out more times than I can count. David participated in so many aspects of this book that it's kind of embarrassing . . . but I'm not embarrassed to say his many contributions were truly and tangibly indispensable to the integrity of this book. Thank you being there.

My past, present and future students, for their enduring ability to inspire me to teach and make beautiful jewelry, semester after semester after semester.

Denise Peck, my technical editor, who came through for me in the eleventh hour; Peternelle van Arsdale, for her friendship, support, and slogging through some projects; Ed and Peggy Strauss, for their friendship, which has meant the world to me; Nina Tegu, fellow Rhode Islander and owner of Studio Hop gallery: Nina was the first to place an order for my jewelry, and gave me the confidence to continue; Margaretta Fox, Heidi Macalle, Susannah Bexley, Donna Estes and Tad San Gabino, Clarissa and Elliot Tricoché, Jennifer Yu, Angela Lowe, and so many other friends who have lent an ear, or a shoulder, or both; my parents Elli and Cal Tillotson; my sister Emma St. Germain; my son Rijk, the only little man on earth with the energy to keep up with me; my parents-in-law Betsy and Palmer Shupe, who have provided me with much design advice and tool talk needed to bring *Chic Metal* to life; and my extended family, who defined the phrase "being there."

index